Modest
# MUSORGSKY

## BORIS GODUNOV

Arranged and Instrumentated by N. RIMSKY-KORSAKOV

An Opera in Four Acts

for Soli, Chorus and Orchestra
with German and English text

VOCAL SCORE

K 06353

# CONTENTS:

## PERSONS OF THE OPERA:

| | |
|---|---|
| Boris Godunow | Baritone |
| Feodor, Xenia, *his children* | Mezzo Soprano · Soprano |
| Xenias, *Nurse* | Low Mezzo Soprano |
| The Duke, Wassili Iwanowitsch Schuiskij | Tenor |
| Andrej Schtschelkalow, *Secretary* | Baritone |
| Pimen, Chronicler, *a Hermit* | Bass |
| The false Dimitrij (called Grigorij) | Tenor |
| Marina Mnischek, *Daughter of the Voyevod, of Sandomir* | Mezzo Soprano |
| Rangoni, *secretly a Jesuit* | Bass |
| Warlaam, Missail, *Vagrants* | Bass · Tenor |
| An Innkeeper | Mezzo Soprano |
| An Idiot | Tenor |
| Nikititsch | Bass |
| A Boyard Guard | Tenor |
| Boyard Chruschtschow | Tenor |
| Lowitzky, Tschernjakowsky, *Jesuits* | Bass |

Single Voices of the PEOPLE (Peasants and Women) Bass (Mitjucha)
Tenor, Mezzo Soprano and Soprano Boyards, Children of Boyards,
Strelitzki, Guards, Captains, Magnates, Polish Ladies, Girls from Sandomir,
Pilgrims, People (Chorus etc.)

Time of the Action · 1598-1605

# Boris Godunow.     Boris Godounow.

Arr. für Gesang und Pianoforte von N. Rimsky-Korsakow.
*Arranged for voice and pianoforte by N. Rimsky-Korsakow.*

M. Moussorgsky. (1872)

## Prolog.     Prologue.

### Erstes Bild.     Scene I.

Hof des Jungfrauenklosters bei Moskau. Den Zuschauern näher befindet sich in der Klostermauer ein mit einem Türmchen versehenes Tor. Volksszene.

The courtyard of the Monastery of Novodievich near Moscow. Near to the spectators is a door in the wall, flanked by a tower. The people assembled.

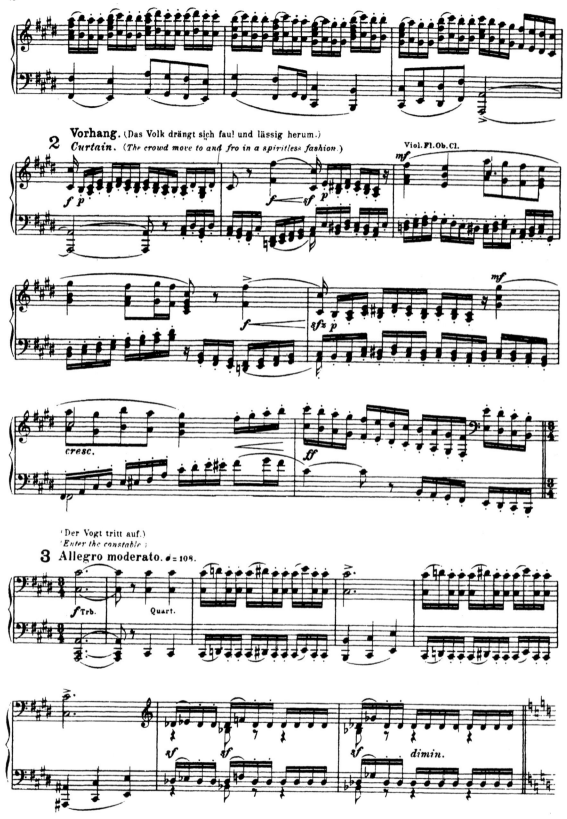

**Vorhang.** (Das Volk drängt sich faul und lässig herum.)
**2 Curtain.** (*The crowd move to and fro in a spiritless fashion.*)

Viol.Fl.Ob.Cl.

(Der Vogt tritt auf.)
(Enter the constable.)

**3 Allegro moderato.** ♩ = 108.

Ten. Ha, ha, ha, ha, ha, ha, ha, ha!

Bass *Ha, ha, ha, ha, ha, ha, ha, ha!*

Ha, ha, ha, ha, ha, ha, ha, ha!
*Ha, ha, ha, ha, ha, ha, ha, ha!*

(Der Vogt tritt auf.)
*(Enter the police officer.)*

(Die Weiber sinken auf die Kniee.)
*(The women kneel.)*

(Das Volk verharrt unbeweglich.)
*(The people are motionless as before.)*

L'istesso tempo. *(Allegro moderato.)* ♩= 108.

**Der Vogt.**
*Police officer.*

(zum Volk)
*(to the crowd)*

cresc.

Was heißt das? dau_ern euch wohl eu_re Keh_len?
*What's this? dumb a_gain? Your throats are ail_ing?*

(Droht mit dem Knüttel.)
*(He threatens them.)*

Wirds bald wohl? O_der sehnt sich eu_er Rücken nach der Knu_te?
*Come, take care! Must I whack you well with this to make you sing out?*

(Dringt auf das Volk ein.)
*(He approaches them.)*

Werd' euch leh_ren, zu ge_horchen!
*Louts, I'll teach you, and quickly!*

(Nach erneuertem Drohen des Vogts.)
*(Under threats from the police officer.)*

**16 Poco animando.**

hört mich an: Bo _ ris ist un _ er _ bitt _ lich! dem we _ hen Ruf des Pa _ tri _
*Mus _ co _ vites, your prayers are vain, he yields not. The ur _ gent wish of all the*

ar _ chen und der Bo _ ja _ ren nicht folgt Bo _ ris und
*Doum _ a, and of the Pa _ triarch, Nought can a _ vail, for Bo _*

weist zu _ rück die Kro _ ne. Es trau _ ert das Land und
*rus de _ clines the King _ dom. O woe to our land, O*

groß ist das Her _ ze _ leid sei _ ner Bür _ ger!
*woe to all Rus _ sia, ye orth _ o _ dox!*

## Pilgerchor.

Die Bühne wird vom rötlichen Licht der untergehenden Sonne beleuchtet. Man vernimmt den Gesang wandernder Pilger. Kirchensänger: Sopran und Alt- Knabenstimmen.)

## Chorus of Pilgrims.

The scene is lit up by the rays of sunset. The pilgrims' song is heard in the distance. (A church choir, with boys' voices, soprano and alto.)

die da hei _ ßet: Auf_ruhr und Gott _ lo _ sig _ keit! Kün_det es der gläub'gen
sen _ sion, sow _ ing dis_cord in our King _ less land! "Proclaim these words to the

die da hei _ ßet: Auf_ruhr und Gott _ lo _ sig _ keit! Kün_det es der gläub'gen
sen _ sion, sow _ ing dis_cord in our King _ less land! "Proclaim these words to the

cresc.

Chri _ stenheit, ihr ___ zum ew' _ gen Heil.
orth _ o _ dox, For ___ sal _ va _ tion waits."

Chri _ stenheit, ihr ___ zum ew' _ gen Heil.
orth _ o _ dox, For ___ sal _ va _ tion waits."

**23** (Amulets unter das Volk verteilend.)
(*Distributing the amulets among the people.*)
Ten. f

Le _ get fest _ li _ che Ge _ wän _ der an, he_bet hoch die Hei _ li _ gen_bil _ der,
Deck your selves with ho _ ly rel _ ics, Let the sac _ red i _ kons be up _ lifted now,

(Treten in's Kloster. Der Gesang erstirbt allmählich.)
(*As they enter in the convent the song gradually dies away.*)

## Zweites Bild.

## Scene II.

Platz im Moskauer Kreml. Den Zuschauern gegenüber, im Hintergrunde der Bühne — die rote Freitreppe der Zarengemächer. Rechts, näher zum Vordergrunde, zwischen der Uspenski- und Archangelskikathedrale – das Volk auf den Knieen liegend. Die Treppenstufen der Kathedralen sind sichtbar.

The courtyard in the Kremlin at Moscow. Facing the spectators, in the background, the Red Staircase leading to the Terem, or apartments of the Tsar. On the right and near the front the people, on their knees, occupy the space between the two Cathedrals of the Assumption and the Archangels. The porches of both churches are in view.

**26** **Vorhang.**
*Curtain.*

(Glockengeläute auf der Bühne.)
(*A great peal of bells on the stage.*)

Die Bojaren ziehen in feierlicher Prozession zur Kathedrale
(*Procession of the Boyards to the Cathedral.*)

Ossia.

lunga

Die Bojaren.
*The Boyards.*

Es le - be der Zar Bo.ris Fe.o.do.rowitsch!
*Long life to the Tsar, Bo.ris Fe. o. do.ro.vich!*

Dem
*Long*

Dem
*Long*

(Boris erscheint und schreitet über die Bühne.)
*(Here Boris appears and walks across the stage.)*

Za.renHeil! Heil der Son.ne, der strah.lend.
*life to thee! To the sun in all splen.dour*

Za.renHeil! Heil der Son.ne, der strah.lend.
*life to thee! To the sun in all splen.dour*

36

Ruhm ___ sei ihm, dem ___ Za ___ ren! Heil dir! Heil dir!
Hail ___ to Bo ris, ___ glo ___ ry! glo ry! glo ry!

Ruhm ___ sei ihm, dem Za ___ ren! Heil dir!
Hail ___ to Bo ris, ___ glo ___ ry! glo ry!

ff

Heil dir! Heil dir! Heil dir! Heil dir! Heil dir! Heil dir!
glo ry! glo ry! glo ry! glo ry! glo ry! glo ry!

Heil dir! Heil dir! Heil dir! Heil dir! Heil dir! Heil dir!
glo ry! glo ry! glo ry! glo ry! glo ry! glo ry!

marcato

f dim. lunga

Andante. ♩ = 72.
32  **Boris.**
Boris.

Wie bang' ist mir... ein selt_sam Angst_ge_
My soul is sad! a_gainst my will strange

Clar.
Cor.
p Cor.                    f          Quart.                    Trb.Cor.

Ruft dann zum Schmaus das Volk her _ bei, ruft al _ le
*And then the peo _ ple all shall feast.* *Aye, ev' _ ry*

her, vom Bettler bis zum Fürst! Heut' sei'n sie all', all'_ mei_ne lie_ben Gä_ste!
*man, from no_ble down to serf; all shall find room, all shall be my hon _ our'd guests.*

(Glockengeläut auf der Bühne.)
*(The bells peal.)*

(Der Zug bewegt sich weiter, zur Archangelskikathedrale.)
*(The procession moves on towards the Cathedral of the Assumption.)*

**34** **Allegro.** ♩ = 120.

Sopr.

Heil dir! Heil dir! Heil dir!
*Glo_ry, glo_ry, glo _ ry!*

Alti

Ten.

Heil dir! Heil dir! Heil dir!
*Glo_ry, glo_ry, glo _ ry!*

Bassi

CORO.

**34**

Allegro. ♩ = 120.

**Das Volk.**
*The People.*

P. G.

Lang' le - be und re - gie - re Zar Bo - ris!
*Long life and glo - ry, fa - ther un - to thee!*

Lang' le - be und re - gie - re Zar Bo - ris!
*Long life and glo - ry, fa - ther un - to thee!*

P. G.

P. G.

(Das Volk drängt sich zur Archangelskikathedrale: die Polizei müht sich Ordnung zu schaffen.)
*(The constable restores order. The people rush towards the Cathedral of the Archangels.)*

**35 Allegro moderato.** ♩= 108.

Heil dir!     Heil dir!
*Glo - ry,     glo - ry!*

Heil dir!     Heil dir!
*Glo - ry,     glo - ry!*

**35 Allegro moderato.** ♩= 108.

41

**44**

(Boris tritt aus der Archangelskikathedrale und schreitet zu den Zarengemächern.)
(Boris leaves the Cathedral of the Archangels and goes towards the Terem.)

Heil! / ry! — Heil dem Zaren! Heil dir! Heil dir!
Glo—ry, glo-ry, glo-ry. glo—ry,

Heil! / ry! — Heil dem Zaren! Heil dir! Heil dir!
Glo—ry, glo-ry, glo-ry, glo—ry,

**Der Vorhang fällt.**
*Curtain.*

Heil dir! Heil dem Za-ren!
glo-ry! Glo-ry, glo-ry!

Heil dir! Heil dem Za-ren!
glo-ry! Glo-ry, glo-ry!

## Erster Aufzug.

### Erstes Bild.

Nacht. Eine Zelle im Tschudowkloster.

## First Act.

### Scene I.

Night. A cell in the Monastery of the Miracle.

**Vorhang.** Pimen schreibt beim Schein eines Kirchenlämpchens. Grigorij schläft.

*Curtain. Pimen is seen writing by the light of a lamp. Gregory asleep.*

**37**

Andante molto. ♩=66.

**Pimen** (im Schreiben innehaltend).
*Pimen. (Resting a while.)*

**38**

Nun ei_ne noch, die al_lerletz_te Kun_de, und mei_ne Chro_nikschreibung ist zu End'.
*Still one more page, the last of all the legends; my chro_ni_cle will then be quite complete.*

(Schreibt.)
(Continues to write.)

Dann ist voll_bracht das Werk, das mir von Gott dem Herrn be_foh_len.
*The task that God as_signed to me, poor sin_ner, is now accomplished.*

46

**Pim.** (hält im Schreiben inne).

**39** **Pim.** (*Pauses in his writing.*)

Der Herr hat nicht um_sonst zum Zeu_gen vie _ ler Jah _ re mich er _ ko _ ren.
*'Twas not in vain God kept me here long years to be His faithful wit_ness.*

Vielleicht wird einst ein ems'_ger Mönch hier fin _ den dies Werk, das ich im
*In fu_ture days, some grave in_dustrious monk shall pro _ fit by my*

Stil _ len hier geschaf_fen, und wird viel_leicht wie ich, beim Schein des Lämp _ chens,
*pi _ ous, nameless la_bours, and, like my _ self, some night he'll light his can _ dle,*

den Staub der Zeit vom Per_ga_men_te wischend, die längst ver_gilb_ten Blät_ter fromm ab_
*the dust of a _ ges from this old parchment shake, ere he transcribe my faith_ful chro_ni_*

schreiben:　　Aus　die sen Blättern wird er sehn die Nach welt　der Hei mat
cle;　　The　grand sons of the orth o dox be liev ers　shall read and

längst　verklung: ner Zei ten Tun.
learn　our land's his tor ic past.

**40** Poco più mosso. ♩=80.

Und neu e Jugend schenkt das Al ter mir.　　Ver-
Tho' old and worn, I seem to live a gain　　When

gangnes zieht vor meinem Geist vor ü ber und steigt her auf wie Wo gen auf dem Meer!...
all the vanished years be fore me pass, the years that on ward roll like ocean's waves;

Einst hat dies Meer ge rauscht er eig nis voll,
and some brought grief and stress and days e vent ful;

doch jetzt ist's still und ru_hig und schweig_sam...
*but now they pass se rene_ly and in si _ lence.*

**41** Andante molto. *(Tempo I.)* ♩=66.

Es graut der Mor_gen schon...
*The dawn is near at hand,*

das Lämpchen will ver_lö_schen...
*my rushlight now is fail_ing...*

Clar.

Nur ei _ ne noch, die al _ ler_letz_te Kun_de...
*Still one more tale, the last of all the le_gends...*

Vcl.

**Grig.**
*Greg.*

Die gan_ze Nacht hindurch hast du geschrieben.
*And thou didst write, all night with zeal un_rest_ing,*

**Animato.**

Mein Schlaf jedoch war
*While my re_pose by*

vol_ler schwe_rer Träu_me: sie pei_nig_ten, ver_wirr_ten mein Ge_müt!
*fear_ful dreams was brok_en: It seemed the fiend did plague my soul in sleep!*

**45 Allegro moderato. ♩=100.**

Mir fräum_te: ei_ne stei_le Trep_pe führt' hoch auf ei_nen Turm mich.
*I'll tell thee: By a stair_case, wind_ing and steep, I reach'd a tow_er.*

Un_ter mir, tief un_ten, Mos_kau lag._
*Thence I saw all Mos_cow at my feet;_*

Wie die A_
*U_as in an*

vor, daß, wenn mich Nachts der Schlummer ü _ ber _ wäl _ tigt     und ich vor _ dem nicht _
*self, outworn with hours of watch_ing, doze or slumb_ er     with_out a pray'r to i_*

ha _ be fromm ge _ be _ tet, daß bö _ se Träu _ me dann     den Schlaf mir rau _ ben. Und
*God, the live _ long night_ I know nor rest, nor peace,     from sin _ ful vi _ sions. In*

trun _ ke _ ne Ge _ la _ ge seh' ich dann,     und wil _ des Kampf ge _ wüh _ le,
*dreams I sit at wild, un _ hall _ ow'd feasts;     I hear the din of batt _ le,*

und sünd' _ ge Lü _ ste tol _ ler Ju _ gend _ zeit...
*Youth's fol _ lies and dis _ trac _ tions all re _ turn.*

mit hin_aus zumKampf? Am Za_ren_hof nicht schwin_gen mei_nen Be_cher?
*know the joys of war;* *to sit at feast with kings at sumptuous ban_quets.*

**48** Pim.
*Pim.*

O mur_re nicht, daß dir die sünd'_ge Welt ver_schlos_sen.
*Re_gret not that the world was ear_ly lost to thee___* Be_

Glau_be mir: die Welt scheintherr_lich uns_ von wei_tem und sü_ße Min_ne
*lieve me: seen from a_far its splendour daz_zles, the love of wom_en*

**A** Moderato assai. ♩=80.

bringt viel Her_ze_leid. O denk, mein Sohn, an all die großen Herrscher...
*lures us from a_far. Yet think, my son, how many Russian monarchs,*

Wer ist hö_her wohl? und dennoch... O, wie oft, wie oft schon
*great tho' they were__ who grea_ter?__ O, in truth, how of_ten*

*pp*

ist es ge_we_sen, daß sie ver_tauschten ih_ren Pur_pur,
*have they most glad_ly put off their pur_ple, dropped their scep_tre,*

die Kro_ne selbst, die güld_ne mit ei_nes Mön_ches här'_ner Kut_te, und
*and doffed their crown and jew_els, put on the poor mon_as_tic hab_it, and_*

**B**

Ru_he fand ihr Herz in stil_ler Klo_ster_zel_le...  Hier, hier in die_ser
*in some hum_ble cell found peace of mind and comfort...  Yes, in this ve_ry*

Zel_le, hier leb_te einst Ky_rill, der heil'_ge Dul_der, ein Got_tesmann... Hier sah den
*cell when ho_ly Cy_ril dwelt with_in its walls,(that man of God)  Here I be_*

Za_ren ich.  Nach_denk_lich, still, saß da I_wan der Vier_te,
*held the Tsar,  The ruth_less Tsar, I_van, grown soft and gen_tle.*

**E.**

Za _ ren gibt es nim _ mer _ mehr! Wir ha _ ben Gott er _ zür _ net, arg ge _ sün _ digt, daß
*more shall we be _ hold his like! Lo, God is wrath with Russia, she has chos _ en as*

wir zum Herr _ scher uns nun ei _ nen Mör _ der aus _ er _ kor'n!
*ru ler and sov'_reign a man of blood, a reg _ i _ cide.*

**Moderato.** ♩ = 92.

**Grig.**
*Greg.*

Schon lang, ehrwürd'_ger Greis schon lan_ge fra_gen wollt' ich
*Long since, O ho _ ly father, to ask this question I have*

dich: wie alt war der Za _ re _ witsch, der er _ mor _ de _ te?
*wished_ What age was he, the Tsa _ re _ vich when they mur_der'd him?*

*) Im Fall einer Einzelaufführung dieser Nummer wird der Abschluß durch den C-moll Akkord *piano* bewerkstelligt.
*On the concert platform, end here, adding the chord of C minor. piano.*

49 Pim.

Er wär' so alt wie du jetzt und wär' nun Zar.
*He would be now your age and should be Tsar to day.*

Doch Gott beschloß es anders. Der blut-ge Fre-vel, den Bo-ris be-
*But o-ther-wise God willed it. 'Twas with this ver-y crime, by Bo-ris*

gan-gen, soll be-schlie-ßen mei-ne Chro-nik nun. Hör', Gri-go-rij! Du
*plan-ned, that to-night I clos'd my chro-ni-cle. Bro-ther Gre-go-ry, Thou*

hast in Wis-senschaft ge-klärt den Geist, drum nimm mein Werk und setz' es fort... ich
*art a man of learn-ing, versed in books, My task to thee I re-le-gate. Set*

ü-ber-geb' es dir beschreibe treu-lich al-les, des-sen du einst Zeu-ge sein wirst:
*down, my son, in un-embellish'd truth All the things of which thou art a wit-ness,*

sei's Krieg, sei's Frieden,
*in war and peace,*
der kür ft'gen Za ren
*in tri bu nals of*

Herr schen.
*state;—*
Pro phe tenspruch und Vor zei chen des Him mels...
*and note all pro phe cies and heav'nly o mens...*

(steht auf und löscht das Lämpchen)
*(Rises and extinguishes his light)*

für mich ist's Zeit, zur Ru he nun zu gehn...
*But as for me, the hour for rest has come...*

**50** Adagio. ♩ = 54.

(Dem Glockengeläut lauschend)
*(Listening to the bell)*

Man ruft zur Mor gen andacht...
*I hear the ma tin bell.*

Cl. Fag.

Tamtam (hinter der Bühne).
*Gong (off the scene).*

Anmerkung: Bei Ausführung mit Klavierbegleitung werden die Tamtamschläge durch das Contra cis wiedergegeben.
*Note: With pianoforte accompaniment, the strokes of the gong mush be rendered by the C sharp of the counter octave.*

## Zweites Bild.
Eine Schenke an der Littauischen Grenze.

## Scene II.
An Inn on the Lithuanian frontier.

## Lied der Schenkwirtin.　The Hostess's Song.

**53** Andantino. (*L'istesso tempo.*) ♩=84.

Schenkwirtin.
Hostess.

Hab' ge_fan_gen ich ei_nen En_te_rich. O du mein
*Once I caught a drake with feathers green and blue. O thou my*

En_te_lein, willst du nicht mein ei_gen sein? Setz', dich En_te_rich, grau_er_ En_te_rich,
*dar_ling drake, come a_gain, my mate so true! Where the pond shines clear, I will take thee dear,*

**54**

Auf den Teich, am U_fer_saum, un_term grü_nen Wei_denbaum. Re_ge, En_te
*There to float and swim at ease Neath the shade of flow'ring trees. Fly a_way, sweet-*

lein, dei_ne Flü_ge_lein, Schwing'dich auf_ frisch und frei, Flie_ge dann zu mir her_bei!
*heart, spread thy wings and soar, High o_ver moor and burn, But to thy poor love re_turn.*

**Poco sostenuto.**

Wer_de ko_sen dich, heiß und min_nig_lich, lie_bes_grau_es En_te_lein, sollst mein trautes
*Weep_ing I will wait, to car_ess my mate, Smooth his feath_ers green and blue, Come a_gain, my*

55

Schätzchen sein! Setz' dich zu mir her, nah', ganz na_he her_
*lo_ver true! Clip, and close_ly hold me, close and clos_er fold me,*

schmie_ge dich an mei_ne Brust, küs_se mich voll sü_ßer Lust!
*I de_sire thy love a_lone, Kiss and make me all thine own!*

Ach, Herrje! Wer kommt denn da?... Lie_be, wer_te Gä_ste!
*Who goes there? Some pas_ser_by! Welcome guests are all friends!*

Hol_la! Kommt doch! Es scheint, sie gehn vorü_ber....
*Ho there! Gone by! Who ever 't was has vanish'd*

**58** Allegretto. ♩=100.

(Warlaam beobachtet Grigorij.)
(Varlaam watches Gregory.)

Andante. ♩=72.

*p trem.*   *cresc.*

**Warl.**
*Varl.*

Sag, Ge_fähr_te, was stimmt dich so trü_be?
*Why so grave and mel_an_cho_ly comrade?*

Sie_he, nun sind an der Grenze wir,   an der Grenze,  zu wel_cher du strebtest so eif_rig.
*Now we are drawing near Po_land   to that frontier Thou long hast been striving to reach.*

**59** **Grig.**
*Greg.*

Erst dann, wenn drü_ben ich bin,  dann erst fin_de ich Ru_he.
*Till I'm in Lith_u_an_ia   there is no peace or safe_ty.*

**59**

6353

# Warlaams Lied. Varlaam's Song.

**Wirtin.**
*Hostess.*

Als ob's kei - nen andern Weg, als nur die Heerstraß hier wei - ter gä - bel!
*They all a - void the high - road and take a by - way! Now, pay at - ten - tion:*

73

Hier gleich links im Wal - de, der schmale
*Choose the left-hand turn - ing. down a long*

Fuß - steig füh - ret bis zur Tschekan'schen Ka - pel - le, den Bach ent - lang
*path - way you will come to the chap - el of Tche - kan, be - side the stream,*

und dann weiter nach Chlopi - no. von dort nach Sai - ze - wo und dort nun
*and from thence on to Khlopi - no; then make for Zai - tse - vo; once there, -*

zeigt je_des Kind dir, wie zur Gren_ze man ge_lan_get. Seit_dem die Hä_scher
*An_y village child will lead you to Lith_u_an_ia.* *These sent_i_nels and*

*poco cresc.*

hier, gibt's kei_ne Ruh' mehr. Tag und Nacht sie schnüffeln und steh_len, wie die
*guards have but one no_tion,* *To op_press poor trav'llers* *and to in_sult us*

*mf*

**Warl.** (gähnt und reckt sich)
**74 Varl.** *(Yawning and stretching.)*

*p*

Ra_ben. Einst kam der Mann
*help_less wo_men.* *There's some one* *Knocks!*

*p*

zum Wirts_haus 'ran, Klopft an die Tü_re an:
*Grease your lock, ock, ock!* *I shay 'tis rust_ty lock,*

*f*

**Wirtin.**
**Hostess.**
(Geht zum Fenster und schaut hinaus.)
*(Goes to the window and gazes out anxiously)*

tuk, tuk, tuk... Wer kommt da noch?
*ock, ock, ock!* *What steps are these?*

*pizz.*

*cresc.* *f* *p*

Wie_der schon die Hä_scher sind's! Schon wie _ der kom_men sie her!
*It is those guards ac _ curs'd! a _ gain they've come here to spy!*

**Warl.**
*Varl.*

's gab mal 'nen Mann,_____ 's war'n gu ter Mann,_____
*No ushe in rea _ shon Shtay here a _ while_____*

(Herein tritt eine Streifwache und beobachtet an der Tür stehen bleibend, die Anwesenden.)
*(The guards enter and watch the Vagabonds.)*

**poco acceler.**

ein her _ zens _ gu _ _ ter...
*Take a ni'sh long shleep!*

**Hauptmann der Streifwache** (tritt von hinten auf Warlaam zu) *ff*
*A Guard. (They stand behind Varlaam.)*

Halt! wer seid Ihr?
*Now then, who are you?*

**poco acceler.**

*cresc.*

**Moderato assai.** ♩ = 84.

**75 Miss.** (demütig)
*Mis. (cringingly)*

Wan _ dern_de Mön _ che, zieh'n ehr_bar uns_re Stra _ße, wan_dern durch die Dör _ fer und
*We are peace_ful her _ mits, humble monks are we_____ And from place to place we go*

**Warl.** (weinerlich)
*Varl. (pitifully)*

Wan _ dern_de Mön _ che, zieh'n ehr_bar uns_re Stra _ße, wan_dern durch die Dör _ fer und
*We are peace_ful her _ mits, humble monks are we_____ And from place to place we go*

**75 Moderato assai.** ♩ = 84.

*mf*

Zeit nah'an die zwan_zig... zwan_zig steht hier ja! Siehst du!
is aged a_bout... twen_ty... Now where's your fif_ty? Look here!

**acceler. poco a poco**

Sein Wuchs ist... sein Wuchs ist mit_tel_groß,
Of med_ium height, ra_ther slim, and his hair

fuchs_ro_tes Haar... ei_ne.... ei_ne War_ze hat er auf der
is chest_nut, on his nose.... his nose.... is a wart, and on his

cresc. poco a poco

Na_se, und ei_ne auf der Stirn... ein Arm ist
face... an_oth_er; His left arm is... left arm... left

(Schaut Grigorij prüfend an.)
(He scrutinizes Gregory.)

**Allegro assai.** ♩ = 144.

kür_zer als der an_dre...
arm is... short_er than his right...

## Zweiter Aufzug.

## Second Act.

Inneres eines Zarengemachs im Moskauer Kreml. Xenia sitzt weinend vor dem Bilde ihres verstorbenen Bräutigams. Der Zarewitsch vor einem, mit Plänen und Karten bedeckten Tische; die Amme ist mit einer Handarbeit beschäftigt.

The interior of the Tsar's appartments in the Kremlin. Sumptuously furnished. Xenia holds the portrait of her lover, and weeps over it. The Tsarevich is reading "The book of great plans." The old nurse is busy with needle-work.

**84 Andante.** ♩ = 66.

**Vorhang.**
*Curtain.*

**Xenia.**
*Xenia.*

Wo weilst du, Bräu_ti_gam, wo bist du, Ge_lieb_ter? In der feuch_ten Er_de,
*Where art thou dear_est? Where art thou my lov_er? In earth's chil_ly bo_som,*

fern vom Hei_mats_lan_de... liegst ein_sam, ver_las_sen im küh_len Gra_be...
*In a far_off coun_try, All lone_ly thou li_est, Be_neath a cold grave_stone.*

du hörst nicht mein Kla_gen, siehst nicht mei_ne Trä_nen, ach_mei_ne hei_ßen um
*Thou see'st not my sor_row, Thou hear'st not my weep_ing, know'st not thy dear one is*

Die Welt ist nicht zu en-ge... ein andrer Bräuti-gam führt dich heim dereinst
*The world is wide, my dear-ie, We'll find an-oth-er woo-er, gay and hand-some,*

**Xenia.**
*Xenia.*

Ach, nein,
*Ah, no,*

als sein E-he-gemahl... wirst bald ver-ges-sen deinen to-ten Bräutigam...
*gra-cious and brave as well. Thy sor-row then will soon be changed to hap-piness.*

nein, nim-mer-mehr! und ist tot er auch, blei-be ihm treu ich
*no, nur sie dear! No, my faith-ful heart, though he be dead, is*

**86**

doch!
*true.*
**Amme.**
*Nurse.*

Sieh' doch! hast ihn kaum ge-seh'n und ver-gehst in Gram...
**86** *Why child! Thou scarce didst know the man, yet dost grieve for him!*

**Amme.**
*Nurse.*

Ei _ ne Maid sich grämt' in Lie _ besschmerz, hatt' ge _ schenkt ei _ nem
*Once a lass _ ie lan _ guisk'd all a _ lone, came a lad a _ woo-ing,*

Bursch ihr jun _ ges Herz. Kam der Bursch nicht mehr zu ihr ins Haus,
*hand _ some and well _ grown; When he proved un _ faith _ ful, quick the maid*

**Recit.**

war's auch mit der hei _ ßen Lie _ be aus... Ach, mein Täubchen,
*Dried her tears and found a swain who stay'd. Hey, my dar _ ling!*

so ist auch dein Kum _ mer! hör' lie _ ber zu, was für ein Lied _ chen ich dir sing':
*put a _ way your sor _ row. Better far for _ get it and list _ en to my tale.*

## Das Lied von der Mücke.    The Song of the Gnat.

sprengt, o weh! auf des Kü_sters Wie_sen_ klee,
*drag_on_fly Through the priest's wide fields pass'd by.*

hüpf_te hin und hüpf_te her, streut' das schö_ne
*Up_set all the cocks of hay. Down the stream they*

Heu ins Meer... Tat's der Mük_ke weh
*sail'd a_way. An_gry grew the gnat,*

um den schö_nen Klee. Nahm ein Holz_scheit, um am fre_chen
*When he look'd on that. Snatch'd a fag_got large and prick_ly*

schrei, eilt' die Wan _ ze _ da her _ bei. Schleppte ei _ ne Schau _ fel
*drop,* *To his aid she came, hop, hop,* *Strove his brok _ en bones to*

**91** Tempo I.

schwer zu der Unglücks _ stät _ te her. Wollt' der Mük _ _ ke
*mend,* *But the gnat was near his end.* *All her ef _ _ forts*

ste _ hen bei, _____ brach sich selbst den Hals ent _ zwei.
*were in vain, _____* *He would nev _ er fly a _ gain.*

poco cresc.

poco rallent.

Mück' und Wanz', o gro _ ße Not! wa _ ren bei _ de mau _ se _ tot.
*Soon the gnat con _ sol'd and shriv _ en, Yield _ ed up his soul to heaven. _____*

## Das „Klatschhändchenspiel."      Clapping game.

**95**

**Feod.** (hört auf zu klatschen.)
**Feod.** (*He ceases clapping.*)

Küsters Frau hat heu - te Nacht
*To the priest's wife one fine day*

ei - nen Spatz zur Welt gebracht. 's war ein rich - ti - ger und ge - wich - ti - ger,
*Cams a sparrow pert and gay, 'Twas a sparrow, true, Quite a young one too,*

reibt die Äu - ge - lein, wetzt sein Schnä - be - lein. Flog der Spatz fort mit Hast
*With a beak, ve - ry long, Yes, a beak sharp and strong. Soon the bird flew a - way*

grad zum Käuz - chen zu Gast, flü - stert ihm leis ins Ohr Wun - der - din - ge:
*With his friend the owl to stay; Whisp'ring low in his ear the owl did say:*

**Amme.**
**Nurse.**

Flü - stert ihm leis ins Ohr Wun - der - din - ge:
*Whisp'ring low in his ear the owl did say:*

**96**

(Feodor und die Amme nähern sich allmählich.)

*(Feodore and the Nurse draw closer together.)*

**Amme.**
**Nurse.** (Klatscht in die Hände.)
*(She claps.)*

Wur_den einst Erb_sen beim Kü_ster ge_dro_schen,die Dresch_fle_gel bra_chen ent_
*Late_ly our deac_on had thresh'd out his bar_ley, His good wife, to dry it In the*

zwei in der Scheu_ne, die Scheu_ne ver_brann_te, hell schlug der
*ov__en must shy it. The ov__en she light_ed, Our deac__on af_*

cresc.

Flam_me Schein dem Kü_ster in das Fen_ster hin_ein.
*fright_ed, Watch'd with wond'ring eyes smoke and leap_ing flames a_riss. The*

**97 Feod.** (Je 2 Schläge auf den Takt.)
**Feod.** *(2 claps in the bar.)*

Hei, wie er_schrak er, kroch schnell un_tern Zu_ber,klemmt ein sich die Oh_ren,
*deac__on, he jump'd in the wat__er_butt light_ly, And closed his ears tight_ly!*

Hei, wie er_schrak er, kroch schnell un_tern Zu_ber,klemmt ein sich die Oh_ren,
*deac__on, he jump'd in the wat__er_butt light_ly, And closed his ears tight_ly!*

**97**

(Xenia und Amme ab.)
(*Exit Xenia and the Nurse.*)
(Boris sieht Xenia mit zärtlichen Blicken nach.)
(*Boris looks at Xenia with tenderness as she goes.*)

zer_streu_e dich mit fro_hem Spie_le.
*for_get thy loss! Find some dis_trac_tion.*

Nun geh', mein Kind!
*Now, go, my child!*

**100**

Feodor.
*Feodor.*

Und du, mein Sohn, ler_nest wohl?
*And thou, my son, what book is this?*

Was ist das?
*An at_las?*

Die
*'Tis*

Kar_te uns_res Rei_ches.
*that of Mus_co_vy,*

Sieh, wie groß ist's...
*all thy king_dom*

von Meer zu Meer.
*from end to end.*

a piacere            in tempo

Schau her doch:
*See, fath_er:*

das ist Mos_kau,
*Here is Mos_cow,*

hier Now_go_rod,
*and Nov_go_rod,*

A

**Rezitativ und Arie.**    **Recitative and Aria.**

Andante. ♩ = 72.

**103** Bor.

Ich hab' er - reicht das Höch-ste. Das sech-ste Jahr schon herr-sche ich in
*I have at - tained to pow - er. Six years have pass'd since first I ruled o'er*

Frie - den,    doch ist's  kein Glück, was mein ge - quäl - - tes Herz er -
*Rus - sia.    But  still  no peace re - turns to  my_____ re - morse - ful*

Più lento. *(Adagio.)* ♩ = 56.

füllt.    Um - sonst ver - kün - det  mir der Ma - gier Spruch ein
*soul.    In vain the seers and  pro - phets all fore - tell long*

Più animato. ♩ = 84.

**104**

lan - ges, glücklich Le - ben    und Re - gie - ren.    Nichts macht mich
*years of life and hon - our,    glad and peace - ful.    Nor life, nor*

froh, nicht Ruhm und Macht noch Eh _ re, der Ju _ bel _ ruf des Volks nicht freut mich mehr.
*pow'r nor glor_y can de_light me, nor plaudits of men_these things give me no joy.*

**105** L'istesse tempo. *(Andantino.)*

In meinem Heim ist mir kein Glück beschie _ den... schon wollt' ich rü _ sten mei _ ner
*My hopes for those most near and dear are blight_ ed; I look'd to make a joy_ful*
*Quart.*

Toch _ ter Hoch _ zeitsmahl _ dem lie _ ben Kin _ de, dem rei _ nen Täub _ chen.
*mar_riage feast for her, my dar_ling daugh_ter, my pure white dove._*

poco allargando

da reißt der Tod hin _ weg den Bräuti _ gam... die Hand des ew' _ gen
*Like lightning death did snatch a _ way her spouse. The heav _ y hand of*

**106** Adagio. ♩ = 56.

Rich _ ters la _ stet schwer, ge _ spro _ chen ist das Ur _ teil mei _ ner See _ le... rings.
*One a_bove doth press up _ on my guilt_y soul, re_quir_ing jus _ tice! A_*

cresc.

um um_hüllt mich grau_si_ges Dun_kel... und nir_gends winkt ein Strahl der Hoff_nung!
round me all is dark_ness un_end_ing, the fu_ture holds nor light nor com_fort.

cresc.

107
Tief schleicht in's_ Herz mir Trüb_sal, es grämt sich und bangt die_
My heart is_ filled with sor_row; and rack'd with des_pair my

p

mü_de See_le, ich fühl' ein heim_lich Zit_tern... die Angst verfolgt mich...
an_guish'd spir_it. Mys_ter_ious ter_rors shake me, aw_ful vis_ions haunt me...

Ich dacht' mit hei_ßen Ge_be_ten zu lin_dern die
In sup_pli_ca_tion I kneel to my Sa_viour, for

p

**108**

bren _ nen_den Qua_len mei_ner See _ _ le,   was hilft al _ le ir _ dische
res _ pite from pain and sharp re _ morse.____   En _ throned in splen_dour, am_

Macht mir un_er_meß _ lich?   Ich,   Ruß _ lands Herr _ scher, ich
bit _ ion's dreams   ac_comp _ lish'd,   I   reign o'er Rus_sia,   yet

**109**

fleh _ te um Trost,   um mil _ de Lind'rungsträ _ nen...   Ver_schwö _ rung
pray __ to God   for tears of   con _ so _ la _ tion.   But God con_

heut',   und Auf _ ruhr mor _ gen, hier   tück' _ sche List   und dort ge_hei_me
demns!   My no _ bles plot   a_gainst   me; the Poles   in se _ cret are con_

Rän _ ke,   Hun _ _ ger, Pest   und e _ lende Ver _ wü _ stung... wie ein wildes
spir _ ing;   fam _ _ ine, pest   and treach _ er_y sur_round   me; while like savage

Dun - kel steht auf vor mir das blut'- ge, to - te Kind.
hours___ the child De - me - trius comes in blood - stain'd shroud.

Flam - men __ __ den Blik __ kes ringt es die Händ __ __ chen,
With eyes di - lat __ __ ed and hands up - rais'd, im -

fleht um Er - bar __ __ men... doch gab es kein Er -
plor __ ing for mer __ __ cy... but mer __ cy was de -

bar - men! Fürch - ter - lich gähnt sei __ ne
pied him! I see the gap - ing wound __ that

Wun __ __ de, grell tönt sein To - des - schrei ins
gleams so red, His cry for ev __ er -

Flügel verleiht es dem denkenden Gei_ste.
*Great are the powers that knowledge will bring thee.*

O hätt' ich doch das Glück dereinst als
*O, might I on ly live to see thee*

Zar'n zu sehn dich, als hoch_er_hab_nen Herrscher Ruß_lands.
*Tsar of Russ_ia, pro_claim'd her one and law_ful rul_er!*

O, mit wel_cher Won_ne, auf Macht und Ruhm ver_zich_tend,
*Ah! then with what glad_ness and scorn of world_ly hon_our*

(Schuiskij tritt auf.)
(*Enter Shouïsky*)

um die_se Seligkeit hin_ge_ben würd' ich mei_nen Scepter!
*I'd fling a_way____ the hea_vy bur_den and fret of statecraft!*

**114** Sohuiskij.
*Shouïsky.* Moderato. ♩=92.

Groß_mächt'_ger Herr und Zar, ich grüß' dich.
*Most no_ble lord and Tsar, thy ser_vant.*

Ha!    du Red_ner, hoch_be_rühmt!    du Rä_delsfüh_rer hirn_verbrannter
Ah,    most el_oquent turn_coat!    Se_duc_er of the stu_pid sheep_like

Men_ge,    du O_berhaupt re_bel_li_scher Bo_ja_ren,
crowd,    ring_lead_er, thou, of my se_di_tious no_bles,

du, des Za_ren_thro_nes    bö_ser Feind,    fei_ger Schuft, drei_fach
en_em_y of Russ_ia    and the Tsar.    Per_jur'd.    doub_ly

mein_ei_di_ger Schur_ke,    schlauer Heuchler du,    Spei_chellek_ker,    Ver_
per_jur'd yet unasham'd,    treas_on_ous flat'rer,    hyp_o_crite,    thou

rä_ter,    den Tod hast du ver_    _die_net!  Be_trü_ger,    Schuft!
maker    of ho_ly wafers    'neath the boyard's robe,__    Snake!

**Schuiskij.** *Skouïsky.*

Erbarm' dich, er-hab'ner Herr und Zar!
*Forgive me, most gracious Lord and Tsar!*

He?
*Eh?*

Hö-re, Fürst:
*Listen, Prince!*

Als sie geschah, die graus'-ge
*When long a-go that ev-il*

Fre-vel-tat in Uglitsch,
*ac-tion was ac-complish'd,*

als hilf-los dort das ar-me Kind
*When, ere his time, the child was sent*

sterben mußt',
*to Heav-en,*

**Schuiskij.** *Skouïsky.*

war je-nes Kind...
*the boy they buried,*

o sag's mir... war's...
*was he in truth*

Di-mi-tri?
*De-me-trius?*

Ja!—
*Yes!—*

Was-si-lij Lwanitsch!
*Vas-si-ly I-va-nich!*

Im Na-men Got-tes, Schuis-kij, ich beschwör' dich
*Now cross thy-self and swear by God to tell me*

ich fleh' dich an... Sprich... sag' die Wahr-heit
*all thou wit-ness'd, All! with-hold no word of*

mir! Du kennst mich als gnäd'gen Zar, doch wisse,wenn du lügst, ich
*truth. Thou know-est my clemen-cy. But if to me thou li-est, I*

schwö-re dir! er-sinn' ich ei-ne Stra-fe dir, so
*prom-ise thee: I will in-vent a pun-ish-ment so*

fürchter-lich, das Zar I-wan im Gra-be selbst vor Grau-sen würd' er-be-ben!...
*aw-ful I-van the Ter-ri-ble him-self would quake to think up-on it!*

**Schuiskij.**
*Shouïsky.*

Gib Ant-wort mir! Nicht schreckt der Tod, viel eh-er dei-ne Un-gnad'.
*Your an-swer,Prince! I fear no tor-ture so much as thy dis-pleas-ure.*

**123** Andante. ♩ = 72.

's war im Dom zu Uglitsch. Vor al_lem Volke sah ich fünf Ta_ge
*In the church at Ouglich, be_fore the peo_ple, Five days I watch'd the*

lang den Leichnam je_nes Kindes. Rings um ihn her_ noch drei_zehn an_dre la_gen,
*bo_dy of the slaughter'd child. And round him lay_ some thir_ty o_ther corpses,*

verstümmelt fürchter_lich, in blut'_gen, schmutz'gen Fet_zen... und es war an
*dis_figur'd, wrapp'd in blood_stained rags for shrouds, they fest_er'd; for in truth, the*

**124**

je_nen schon zu spü_ren die Ver_we_sung. Doch das Ge_
*bo_dies all did cry a_loud for bur_ial. The face of*

sicht des Za_rensohns war rein und wie ver_klärt,_
*one, the boy Di_mit_ri, was still as fair as in his life,_*

doch fürchterlich, klaffend gähnt die To - deswun - de. Auf sei - nen rei - nen
though red and deep a gash did show, his throat en - cir - ling. Yet on his lips, so

dimin.

Lip - pen spiel - te ein wun - der - sa - mes, herr - lich Lä - cheln, es
in - no - cent, a won - der - ful an - ge - lic smile was play - ing. It

pp

schien, als ob das Kind in sei - nem Bett - chen schlumm're süß,— ge - kreuzt die
seem'd as though he slum - ber'd in his cra - dle, a babe once more.— His hands were

pp

cresc.

Händchen und mit der Rech - ten hielt es fest ein Spielzeug noch...
fold - ed, but still he grasped the toy he last had play'd with.

**Bor.**
**Bor.**

Nicht wei - ter!...
En - ough, Prince!

cresc.

(Gib° Schuiskij ein Zeichen sich zu entfernen. Schuiskij geht, sich nach Boris umschauend. Boris sinkt in einen Lehnsessel.)
*(Boris makes a sign to dismiss Shouïsky. As the latter withdraws he glances back at Boris, who sinks into his arm chair.)*

**125** L'istesso tempo. ♩ = 72.

## Die Uhr mit Glockenspiel.
(Boris allein.)

## Scene with the chiming clock.
(Boris alone.)

**126** Recit.

Huh! war das schwer! der A-tem geht mir aus...
*Ouf! I suf-fo-cate! Scarce can I draw my breath!*

Tempo (*moderato*)

Ich
*I*

fühl-te, wie das Blut mir sie-dend stieg zum Kopf und wie-der kehrt' zum
*feel that all my blood has rush'd in-to my brain; it stays there and still*

Her-zen.
*throbs.*

O, bös' Ge-wis-sen, wie ent-
*O conscience, remorse-less, how*

Volks - wil - le war es... hörst du, Kind...
*The peo - ple all will'd it! Child, be - gone...*

128

allarg. poco a

Herr mein Gott!
*God, a - bove!*

Der Du nicht den Tod des Sün - ders willst, o sei mir gnä - dig!
*Who de - sir - eth not the sin - ner's death, have mer - cy up - on me,*

Der Vorhang fällt.
*Curtain.*

poco ritard.

Er - barm'dich dei - nes Knechts Bo - ris.
*Yea, on me, the guilt - y Tsar Bo - ris!*

## Dritter Aufzug.

### Erstes Bild.

#### Chor der Mädchen von Sandomir.

Gemach der Marina Mnischek im Schloß zu Sandomir. Marina
sitzt vor dem Spiegel und lauscht den Mädchen.

## Third Act.

### Scene I.

#### Chorus of Maidens of Sandomir.

The room of Marina Mnishek, where she is discovered at her
toilette. The girls amuse her with their songs.

Soprani.
Am U - fer___ der Wei - chsel, im Schat - ten___
By Wis - la's___ blue wa - ters, be - neath an___

- der Wei - den, da weiß ich ein Blüm - lein, schneeweiß und süß - duf - tend.
- old wil - low, a flow' - ret is bloom - ing with pet - als like snowflakes

süß - duf - tend.
like snow - flakes

In spie_geln _ de Flu_ten schaut lä _ chelnd es nie_der, draus lacht ihm  sein hol_des
*All day in __ the mir_ror of glass _ y __ clear wa_ter, half dreaming  she watches*

**131**
*dolce*

Bild lieb_lich  ent_ge_gen.
*her beau _ ty  re _ flec_ted.*

*dolce*

**131**

*pp Quart.*

schwebt luf_tig __ und leicht ein Schwarm glit_zern _ der Fal_ter, sich wie_gend  im Reigen.
*and flash_ing __ in sunshine a my_riad __ bright in_sects, with wings so __ gaily painted.*

Zur Freu — de von ganz San_do_mir blühet herr — lich die hold_sel'.
*The pride and the glad_ness of all San_do_mir, and the flow'r of_*

dim.

**135**

_ge Maid. Nicht we_nig hoch_ed_le und glän_zen_de Her_ren
_our land. *How man_y gal_lants are lur'd by such_ lov_li_ness!*

**135**

Be_fan_gen nei_gen sich vor ih_rem hol_den Liebreiz, ihr lieb_li_chesLächeln
*They flock to a_dore her, and strive to win our fair maid, But no_ne are ac_cept_ed*

8..............................
etc.

Quart.

*mf*

*pp*    *pp*

glückse - lig ___ er - haschend, zu Fü - ßen ___ ihr schmachtend, in Sehn - sucht ___ ver - geh - end
*Her smiles they ___ are priceless, to kneel at ___ her foot - stool is count - ed ___ an hon - our.*

**136** *dolce*

Doch un - ser - jung' Fräulein lacht schelmisch dar - ü - ber, lacht ü - ber ___ ihr Schmachten, ihr flam - men
*Our love - ly ___ princess has no fan - cy ___ for woo - ers, She list - ens ___ and mocks when with pas - sion*

**136**

*poco riten.*

___ des Wer - ben; will nicht er - hö - ren ihr Fle - hen und ihr Seuf - zen, ihr Seuf - zen.
*they court her, and scorn - ing to wed, on their vows of de - vo - tion looks cold - ly.*

*poco riten.*

*morendo*

**L'istesso tempo.** ♩ = 96.
**137** Marina.
Marina.

Hört auf nun! Das schö - ne Fräu - lein sa - get Dank euch für
*E - nough, girls! Your beau - ti - ful prin - cess now thanks you for*

eu- re lie- ben Wor- te,  für den Ver- gleich mit  je- nem schö- nen Blüm- lein,
*all your pret- ty speech- es,*  *com- par- ing her to*  *frag- ile, haugh- ty blos- soms,*

das so hold und schnee weiß.  Doch nicht be- hag- te Pan- na Mni- schek  das
*Whit- er than the snow- flakes;*  *But still, your prin- cess is not hap- py.*  *What*

schmeichle- ri- sche Lob- lied  und die ab- geschmack- te, fa- de An- spie- lung
*use, your ad- u- la- tions,*  *Your de- vo- tion, your unmean- ing words of flat- 'ry?*

**138**

auf hoch- ed- le Her- ren,  die täg- lich scha- ren- wei- se  zu ih- ren Fü- ßen lie- gen,
*All this pack of lov- ers,*  *these gild- ed youths and gallants,*  *who kneel to me and languish,*

in Sehn- sucht sich verzehrend.  Nein, nicht sol- che Lie- der wünscht sich
*and crave for tri- fling favours!*  *Nay, Ma- rin- a asks not songs of*

molto rit.  Allegro risoluto. ♩=144.

pp molto rit.  sf  f  p. dim.

poco riten.

Pan _ na Mni _ schek, will kein Lob _ lied ih _ rer Schön _ heit von euch hö _ ren.
*love and dal _ liance,* *Nor to hear her beau _ ty prais'd by maids who serve her.*

**139** **Tempo I.** *(Allegretto.)* ♩= 96.

Singt ihr lie _ ber sol _ che Lie _ der, die als Kind sie einst ge _ sun _ gen.
*Sing the songs my nurse once taught me, Won _ drous songs of days de _ part _ ed.*

Hel _ den _ lie _ der, Sie _ ges _ lie _ der, die von Po _ lens Grö _ ße re _ den und von tap _ fren
*Songs of War _ riors, Songs of conquest, Songs that ring with Po _ land's glo _ ry; Sing of times when*

poco ritard. **Allegro risoluto.** ♩= 114.

Po _ len _ jungfrau'n, von ge _ schlag'_ nen Po _ len _ fein _ den. Das ist's, was ich hö _ ren möch _ te,
*maids were read _ y For their land to per _ ish bravely. These are songs to please your mis _ tress,*

riten. molto **Tempo I.** *(Allegretto.)*

sol _ che Lie _ der hör' ich ger _ ne! Nun ge _ het!
*They a _ lone con _ sole her dull _ ness. Now leave me!*

*p colla parte*

*) Anmerkung. Wenn die folgende Arie der Marina einen Ton höher (in fis-moll) ausgeführt werden soll, so bedient man sich hierzu als Übergang der (von Ziffer 140 an) kleingedruckten Musik.

*If it is desired to transpose Marina's air, which follows, a tone higher (in f♯ minor) the bars in small notation may be used as a connecting passage.*

Arie der Marina.  Marina's Air.

**Moderato.** ♩=96.

**141**

Marina.

Lang _ wei _ lig ist's mir, ach, wie lang _ wei _ lig!
*Ah, poor Ma _ ri _ na! Ah, how dull is life!*

**Alla mazurka.** ♩=144.

Wie so ö _ de, schal und fa _ de ziehn die Ta _ ge hin sich, wie so in _ halts leer.
*Life is emp _ ty, life is drea _ ry, long the days and wea _ ry, cheer _ less, grey and flat,*

ein _ för _ mig! Nicht ver _ mag ein gan _ zer Schwarm von Für _ sten, Gra _ fen,
*Sing Heigh ho! All the host of men who woo me, knights and wealth _ y*

Rit _ tern mir zer _ streu'n die Lan _ ge _ wei _ le!
*mag _ nates, can _ not make ex _ ist _ ence bright _ er!*

mein Za_re_witsch, mein Di_mi_tri, du, mein Heiß_ge_lieb_ter!
*My Tsa_re_vich, my Di_mi_tri, I will teach thee cour_age!*

**Poco più lento.**

Pan_na Mni_schek nicht be_frie_digt all die lau_e Herz_er_gießung der ver_lieb_ten
*For Mar_i_na long has wear_ied, sought by lov_ers shy and tep_id, Youths who on_ly*

poco cresc.

**Animando.**

Her_renschar, die fa_den Re_den der Magna_ten. Pan_na Mni_schek sehnt nach Ruhm sich,
*dream of pas_sion, worthy mag_nates vain and pompous. But Mar_i_na longs for glo_ry,*

**146 Tempo I. (alla masurka).** ♩= 144.

Pan_na Mni_schek lechzt nach Herrschaft.
*But Mar_i_na craves for pow_er!*

Werd' als Za_rin
*On the roy_al*

auf dem Thron der Mos_ko_wi_ter sit_zen, und in gold durch_wirk_tem Pur_pur
*throne of Mos_cow I would queen it proud_ly, robed in pur_ple, deck'd with jew_els,*

*) Anmerkung. Der plötzliche Eintritt der Quinte F-C bleibt unverändert, einerlei in welcher Tonart die vorgehende Arie ausgeführt wird.

The sudden entry on the fifth F-C must not be altered whatever the key in which the preceding air has been sung.

**152**

Mar.

wel _ che Sünd'!... Hoch _ wür _ den, o wie ent _ setz _ lich habt Ihr ver _
*This is sin! My fath _ er, what great temp _ ta _ tions dost thou un _*

füh _ ret mei _ ne sün _ di _ ge und un _ er _ fahr _ ne, flat _ ter _ haf _ te See _ le...
*fold be _ fore the change _ ful, err _ ing heart of thy weak daught _ er Mar _ t _ na?*

**153** Allegretto. ♩= 112.

Nein, nicht mir wird es ge _ lin _ gen, mir, die ich gewöhnt an Lust und Freuden, nein, nicht mir ist
*Nay, I love the world too dear _ ly, all its rev _ el _ ry, its wealth and brightness. Not for me this*

es beschieden, Got _ tes Leh _ re zu verkün _ den. Nicht ver _ mag ich's...
*loft _ y mis _ sion, to implant the Faith in Russ _ ia. Spare my weak _ ness!*
Rang.
*Rang.*

*lunga*

*lunga*

So
*Thy*

Bis _ wei _ len stel _ le dich zor _ nig, dann wie _ der sei wäh _ le _ risch, lau _ nisch,
*Use ev' _ ry art that thou know _ est* *and play the light, fick _ le wo _ man;*

bis _ wei _ len zärtlich und schmeichelnd... Mit al _ len nur denk _ ba _ ren Kün _ sten
*or try per _ suasion and flat _ 'ry;* *try sub _ tle de _ ceit and sug _ ges _ tion.*

sollst um _ gar _ nen ihn, mußt be _ strik _ ken ihn,
*Lure and lead him on,* *catch and keep him fast.*

und, wenn er dann ermat _ tet zu Fü _ ßen dir sinkt in un _ säg _ li _ cher Won _ ne,
*Then, when at thy feet _ he wor _ ships, lost in love _ rap _ ture, by pass _ ion con _ quer'd,*

und harrt dei _ ner Wünsche... For _ d're von ihm dann den
*read _ y for thy bidding,* *Wring out his oath to ad _*

du hast    mein Herz er _ fül _ _ let!...
*this voice    can fill    my    heart!*

**161** Arpa.

*f dimin.*

*p*

*mf*

*mf    dim.*

**162** Dimitri.
*Demetrius.*

Ob du wohl kommst, Ge_lieb_te mein? mein
*Be lov_ed, wilt thou come to me? As*

Täubchen, mein weißes, mein leicht_be_schwingtes du! Hast wohl ver_ges_sen schon den kühnen
*wing_eth a dove to her mate will thou come to me? Or hast thou for_gotten thy fal_con un_*

Fal_ken du, der nun in Sehnsucht heiß sich um dich ver_zehrt? mit hol_dem
*daunt_ed, who ev_er pines for thee, yearns and lan_guish_es for ten_der*

Lie_besgruß, sü_ßem Ko_se_wort, Ma_ri_na, lin_dre du mei_ne quä_lend'
*greet ings and words of wel__come? O, come my la_dy, for thou a_lone canst*

Her — zenspein! heal my pain! trem. Ma — ri_na... Ma — ri_na!

Ma — ri — na!... Ma — ri — ná!

**163**

sempre tremolando

Gib Antwort! Answer! O, gib

pp cresc. poco a poco

Ant — wort! ri — na! O, komm', o komm', ich har_re dein, ich O come, o come, I wait for thee, I

**Dim.**
**Dem.**

O,— wenn du nur nicht lügst, wenn's nicht der Sa_tan ist, der mir die_se wunder_sa_men
*Ah!— were thy words but true! Could I be_lieve thee, nor feel all that thou say'st inspir'd by*

**Meno mosso.**

Wor_te spricht... o, dann werd' ich sie er_he_ben vor'm gan_zen
*Sa_tan. I would flee a_way with my dar_ling, my fair white*

rus_si_schen Land, wer_de führen sie mit mir auf den Za_ren_thron, ih_re
*dove, far a_way, to the land of Rus_sia would I go, and set her on high, on the*

*a piacere*

Zau_berschönheit blen_den wird das recht_gläub'ge Volk!... Du Dä_mon!
*Tsar's own throne, and all the folk should wor_ _ship her!... Foul tempt_er!*

**a tempo**

wie ein nächt_lich' Dieb, so schleichst du in's Herz mir, du hast mir dies Be_
*Like a thief in the night thou pier_cest my soul's most in_ward, se_cret*

*cresc.*

Rang. kennt_nis schlau ent_ris_sen, du lügst! Ma_ri_na liebt mich nicht!
Rang. sanc_tu_ary to rob it. Ma_ri_na loves not me. Priest, thou liest!

Ich, ich sollt'
I, lie to thee?

**Moderato assai.**

be_lü_gen dich, Za_sewitsch? Um dich al_lein sie grämt und härmt sich Tag und
Where_fore should I lie, Tsar_e_vich? I tell thee, day and night Ma_ri_na thinks and

*colla parte*

Nacht in hei_ßer Lie_bes_sehn_sucht, täglich träumt sie in nächtli_cher Stil_le von
dreams of thee, a_lone in si_lence; in the calm noc_turn_al wat_ches her

dei_ner hoh_en Zu_kunft. O, wenn du wirk_lich lieb_test sie,
thoughts a_bide with thee. O, didst thou love her bet_ter, and

o, wenn du wüß-test ih-re Qua-len,
*could'st thou but guess the pangs she suf-fers,*
hör-test den Spott der Mag-
*poor proud and high-bred*

na-ten,
*la-dy,*
hä-mi-schen Neid ih-rer Frau-en,
*no-ting the whis-pers of mal-ice,*
bos-haf-tes Zi-scheln,
*the smiles of mock'-ry*

lee-res Ge-re-de von heim-li-chen Stelldicheins, heim-li-chen Küs-sen,
*gos-sip and hints of meet-ings in se-cret, light talk of kis-ses,*

all die-se un-er-träg-li-che Krän-kung, dann wür-dest du glau-ben mir schon, und
*trif-les that wound a sen-si-tive soul.— O didst thou but know all she feels, thou*

würdest nicht wei-sen von dir mei-ne Wor-te, Lü-ge nicht nennen du würdest die Qua-len Ma-
*ne'er wouldst upbraid me nor brand me a li-ar. True, ah, too true— the in-sults endur'd by Ma-*

**Dim.**
**Dem.**

O, schwei-ge! bit _ ter trifft mich dein Vor _ wurf; doch zu lang' mußt' ver-
E nough! Cease to hurl re _ proa _ ches. Far too long have I

ri _ na's.
ri _ na.

ber-gen ich mein Glück vor den Men _ schen! Ma _ ri _ na wer _ de treu ich
hid _ den from the world all my rap _ ture! I will de _ fend Ma _ ri _ na's

dim.

schützen, ich wer _ de zücht'gen die Ver _ mess'nen,
hon _ our, and deal with these pre _ sump _ tuous no _ bles;

zur blut'gen Re _ chen _ schaft ziehn die Ver _ läumder, ver _ lachen werd'ich all ih _ re
frustrate the sland _ ers and tricks of their wo _ men, and laugh to scorn their pit _ i _ ful

Bosheit, und öf-fentlich werd' ich, vor al-len Mag-na-ten, mich wer-fen der hol-den Ma-
malice; be-fore the whole false-tongued as-semblage of no-bles I will de-clare bold-ly my

ri-na zu Fü-ßen und ihr mei-ne hei-ße Lie-be ge-ste-hen, wer-de sie
love for Ma-ri-na. I'll kneel at her feet and humb-ly im-plore her on my great

Rang. fleh-ent-lich bit-ten, zu sein mein sü-ßes Weib, mei-ne herr-li-che Za-rin!...
Rang. pas-sion to look without scorn; pray her to wed me, and be my queen!

Der heil'-ge
May Saint Ig-

Du, der du der Welt ent-sagt hast, der
Thou, who hast re-nounc'd the world, thou,

Ig-naz helf' dir da-zu!
na-tius pros-per thy suit!

Meno mosso.
Rang.
Rang.

hoch,     den nicht zah_len ich würd'.          Ein from_mer,   de_muts_vol_ler Die_ner des
may,     I  will pay thee thy price.             My son,   I  am  a  hum_ble  priest  who

himm _ li _ schen Herrn,     der stünd_lich nur   ans Wohl des Nächstendenkt und an die
lives  but  by pray'r,     and med _ i _ tates   on  death___  and judgment,  on  the

ew' _ ge Ver_gel_tung  am jüng_sten  Ge_richt___  ihn lockt keinPreis,ihn lockt kein Gold...
re _ tri _ bu_tion  re _ served for  that day   which comes when no man looks for it.

Sieh:     ein solcher bin ich,   und mich kön_nen kei_neSchätze lok_ken hier auf Er_den!
Yea,     to car_nal pleasures  long in_diff'rent, what have I to  do with worldly treasures?

ri - na, laß mich, um - ar - men sie...
*ri - na, my queen, my be - lov - èd...*

Was ist dir?
*What say'st thou?*

Rang.
*Rang.*

Verbirg'dich, Dmi - tri!
*Tsar - e - vich, hide thyself!*

Ich
*The*

hör', es kommt hier - her ein Hau - fen ze - chender Mag - na - ten.
*ban - quet's done, and see, how yon - der comes a group of Mag - nates.*

O flieh', Za - re - witsch,
*Begone, Tsar - e - vich,*

Dim.
*Dem.*

Laß sie kommen, wer - de sie emp - fan - gen dem Rang ge - mäß mit al - ler
*Let them come then, I will bid them welcome, to each ac - cor - ding to his*

ich beschwöre dich, o geh'!
*I im - plore thee, be - gone!*

Eh - re
*me - rits.*

Be - sinn' dich, Za - re - witsch! Bringst dich selbst ins Ver - der - ben, ver - ra - test Ma - ri - na... O
*Be cau - tious, Tsar - e - vich, wouldst thou risk thy - self then, and lose thy Ma - ri - na? Go,.*

cresc.

## Polacca mit Chor.

(Dimitri verbirgt sich hinter den Bäumen.)

(Aus dem Schlosse kommt eine Schar Gäste.)

## Polacca with Chorus.

(Dimitri conceals himself among the trees.)

(A crowd of guests come out of the castle.)

**165**

Tempo di polacca. ♩ = 100.

**167**

**188** Marina (am Arm eines alten Magnaten;.
*Marina (on the arm of an elderly nobleman).*

Nein, nicht glaub' ich Eu _ ren sü_ßen Wor_ten, Eu _ re hei_ßen
*Nay, my lord, I scarce believe your pro_tests; all your vows of*

Lie‿besschwüre sind ver‿geb‿‿lich!
*love e‿tern‿al can‿not touch‿‿me!*
Nim‿mer‿mehr wird's Euch ge-
*Nev‿er, sir, will your soft*

lin‿‿gen mich, Ma‿ri‿na, zu be‿tör'n.
*speech‿‿es, have the pow'r to de‿ceive‿me.*

(gehen vorüber)
*(they pass on)*

**Ten.** 169
Bald wird un‿ser sein das Reich der Mos‿ko‿wi‿ter,
*We shall sure‿ly cap‿ture Mos‿cow, bag and baggage!*

**CORO.** Bassi.

**169**

Wer‿den die Bar‿ba‿ren
*Lead our Rus‿sian cap‿tives*

Ih‿re Krie‿ges‿hee‿re wer‿den bald wir tre‿ten
*How we'll send Bo‿ris and all his squadrons fly‿ing!*

bald ge‿fan‿gen neh‿men! Tre‿ten wir wer‿den ihr
*home to you fair la‿dies, We will drive them like the*

Tre‿ten wir wer‿den ihr
*We will drive them like the*

säumt _____ nicht län - ger mehr.
*Tsar* _____ *Bo_ris is ours!*

ziehn!          Auf!          Vor_wärts, auf den Feind!
*March,*        *march!*      *Tsar Bo_ris is ours!*

Auf!            Auf!          Vor_wärts, auf den Feind!
*March,*        *march!*      *Tsar Bo_ris is ours!*

*poco cresc.*

**171**

198

(Marina und die Gäste treten ins Schloß.)
(Marina and the guests re-enter the castle.)

L'istesso tempo. ♩ = 100.

**175** Dimitri. (allein)
Demetri. (alone)

Der schlau _ e Je_su_it      hält mich fest in sei_nen zä_hen Teu_fels_
*Vile and craft _ y Jes _ u_it.*      *All too close_ly hath he caught me in his*

kral _ len,    und nur von wei_tem, flüch_tig nur    ge_lang es mir, Ma_
*tram _ mels!*    *For one brief mo _ ment, far a _ way,*    *I caught a glimpse of*

ri _ na zu er_blik_ken und ih_rer dunk_len Au _ gen Zau_berglanz ganz heimlich
*my di_vine Ma _ ri _ na, and fur_tive_ly I watch'd the glance and gleam of her bright*

nur zu spü_ren.      Wie schlug mein Herz so wild doch, ach! und so stürmisch
*eyes like star_beams.*      *My heart was throb_bing wild_ly.*    *Ah, with what ard_our,*

daß ich na‿he war da‿ran mich los‿zu‿rei‿ßen, den un‿ge‿bet'‿nen Schutzherrn fort‿zu‿
*With what heat I longed to strike a blow for freedom, and slay my hat‿ed, un‿in‿vi‿ted*

ja‿gen, den geist‿li‿chen Be‿ra‿ter. Wie sein Ge‿schwätz so
*guard‿ian, my spi‿ri‿tual fa‿ther! The while he talk'd un*

wi‿der‿lich, und sein Ge‿red' voll Arg‿list bis zur Frechheit! Am
*ceas‿ing‿ly and pour'd forth streams of lies and emp‿ty phra‿ses, I,*

Arm des prah‿le‿ri‿schen, al‿ten Po‿len schritt stolz wie ei‿ne Kö‿ni‿
*stand‿ing by, be‿held my love‿ly la‿dy go past up‿on the arm of*

gin Ma‿ri‿na: ein herr‿lich Lä‿cheln um die sü‿ßen Lippen, wohl
*some vain lordling; I saw Ma‿ri‿na sweet‿ly smile up‿on him. and*

flü_ster_te die Hol_de von zar_ter Min_ne, von brünst'ger Sehnsucht,
whis_per charming spee_ches, ten_der and low;_ Perchance she prom_is'd

*a piacere*

von sü_ßem E_he glücke... als Weib die_ses see_len_lo_sen Wüstlings! da ihr das
to be his own, his bride... Ma_ri_na! to wed a heartless rake! When fate more

Schick_sal glü_hen_de Lie_bes_won_nen bie_tet, die gold'_ne Kro_ne
kind would give her true love and gladness and glor_y, a crown of gold, a

cresc.

*Più mosso.*

und den Pur_pur_man_tel!... der Teu_fel hol's! Geschwind die
throne and robes of pur_ple! Nay, God for_bid! Without de

stäh_lern Waffen_rü_stung! den Helm, das Schwert umgür_tet,
lay, I'll don my ar_mour! My helm, my gleaming fal_chion,

und sich in hei‿ßer Schlacht er‿kämp‿fen den Thron!
*mount___ in tri‿umph the throne of my fa‿thers!*

**Meno mosso.**

Marina (tritt in den Garten)
*Marina (enters the garden)*

Dim.
*Dem.*

Di‿mi‿tri! Za‿re‿witsch! Di‿mi‿tri! Sie ist's,___
*Di‿mi‿tri! Tsa‿re‿vich, Di‿mi‿tri! 'Tis she___*

(geht ihr entgegen)
*(going towards her)*

espr.

Ma‿ri‿na! O,___
*Ma‿ri‿na! Thou?___*

mein sü‿ßes Täub‿chen, o, bist du end‿lich da!
*O my be‿lov‿ed, my beau‿ti‿ful prin‿cess!*

Allegretto. ♩ = 96.

Nicht für Lie_bes_tän_de_lei und nicht um lee_rer Re_den wil_len
*Nay.* *I came not here to speak* *of .lov_er's sighs and fool_ish fan_cies,*

bin ge_kom_men ich: Bist al_lein du, magst du träu_men, magst in
*oth_er thoughts are mine.* *Thou, in lone_ly hours of wait_ing may'st con*

Lie_be du ver_gehn, so viel du willst. Selbst die al_ler_größ_ten
*sole thy_self with dreams of love and me.* *There! Thou need'st not feign sur*

Dim. Dem.

Ma_ri_na!
*Ma_ri_na!*

Op_fer könn_ten mich nicht rüh_ren, und sei's dein Tod so_gar vor lau_ter
*prise, 'tis well that thou should'st know:* *I ne'er could love thee ev_en didst thou*

poco rit.

Lieb' zu mir. Sag', wann ziehst du in Moskau ein als
*die for me.* *But when shall Mos_cow see thee reign as*

colla parte

**180** Allegretto. ♩ = 96.
Mar. *Mar,*

all dem Ent_zük_ken des mächt'gen Lie_beszaubers? Na_tür_lich! Auch in ei_ner
*ar_dent car_ess_es all love's bewitching pow'r? Oh, spare me! In some humble*

e_lend'Hüt_te wür_den Beid' wir glück_lich sein, was ist uns an Ruhm ge_le_gen?
*lit_tle cot_tage thou and I shall dwell in bliss; what to us are thrones and kingdoms?*

**Alla mazurca.** ♩ = 144.

wenn al_lein schon's Lie_ben satt uns macht! Wenn Ihr nun, Za_re_witsch, der Lie_be
*We can live for love and love a_lone! If in truth, Tsa_re_vich, a life like,*

nur be_dür_fet, so könn_tet Ihr in Mos_kau nicht we_nig Frau_en fin_den,
*this delights thee, thou wilt sure_ly find in Mos_cow a host of wil_ling damsels,*

die schön sind und ro_sig und gar be_geh_renswert.
*all love_ly, all ro_sy, with hair___ of sa_ble hue!*

poco ritard.

**Alla mazurka.** ♩= 144.

**183**

O, mein Traut-ge-sel — — le, quäl'dich nicht umsonst mit
*Rise, poor fool-ish lov-er and grieve no more,since all thy*

Flehn und Seuf — zen. O, steh' auf, du Ar — mer, wie du leid mir tust,
*pray'rs are use-less. Rise, poor suf-f'ring mar-tyr. Ah! how I pit-y thee!*

du mein Ge-lieb-ter! Bist vor lau-ter hei-ßer Lie-be zu Ma-ri-na
*My gent-le friend. I grieve to see thee brok-en heart-ed, lost for love of*

ganz erschöpft schon...Tag und Nacht von ihr nur träumst du, hast dar-ü-ber ganz ver-ges-sen,
*thy Mari-na; Night and day of her thou dreamest, Hast thou then thy throne for-got-ten,*

daß ja Zar du wer-den wolltest... Fort! du Va-ga-bund du!
*ceas'd to think of Tsar Bo-ris?__ Hence, be-gone im-post-er!*

**185** Moderato alla breve. ♩=84.

strömt mir zu das Volk aus al _ _ len Gau _ en; schon
*Russ _ ian friends, from ev' ry side_____ are flock _ ing; to _*

mor _ gen geht's hin _ aus zum blut _ gen, hei _ ßen Kamp _ fe,
*mor _ row sees me lead my val _ iant troops to but _ tle.*

wie _____ ein Ad _ ler kühn, so stür _ me ich nach Mos _ kau zum
*War _ riors tried and true. We'll march up _ on the Krem _ lin, for*

Za _ _ ren thron, den mir das Schicksal beut!
*fate hath de _ creed, that I mount my fa _ ther's throne!*

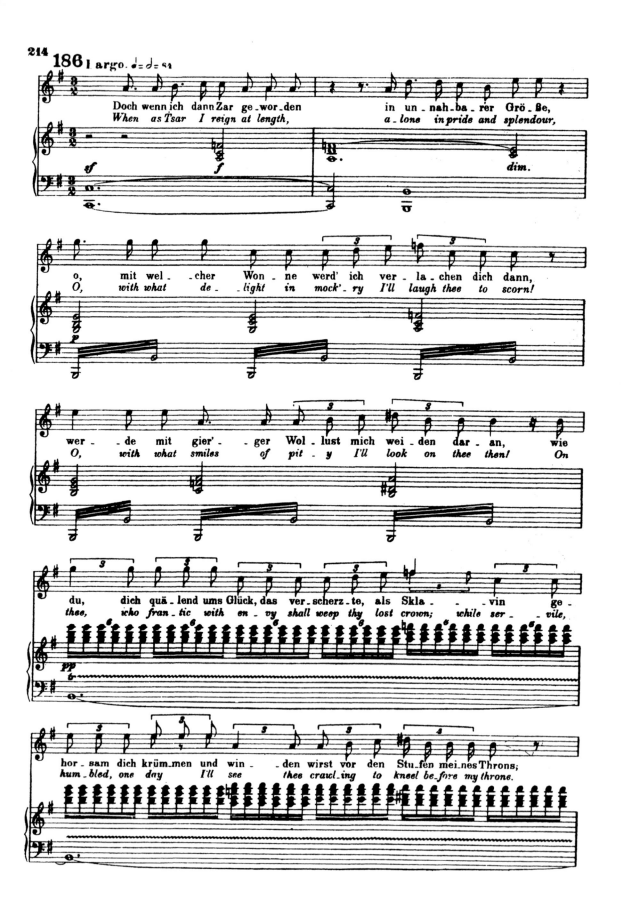

**186** Largo.

Doch wenn ich dann Zar ge _ wor _ den    in un _ nah _ ba _ rer Grö _ ße,
*When    as Tsar I reign at length,    a _ lone in pride and splendour,*

o,    mit wel _ _ cher Won _ ne werd' ich ver _ la _ chen dich dann,
*O,    with what de _ _ light in mock' _ ry I'll laugh thee to scorn!*

wer _ _ de mit gier' _ ger Wol _ lust mich wei _ den dar _ an,    wie
*O,    with what smiles of pit _ y I'll look on thee then!    On*

du,    dich quä _ lend ums Glück, das ver _ scherz _ te, als Skla _ _ vin ge _
*thee,    who fran _ tic with en _ vy shall weep thy lost crown; while ser _ _ vile,*

hor _ sam dich krüm _ men und win _ _ den wirst vor den Stu _ fen mei _ nes Throns;
*hum _ bled, one day I'll see    thee crawl _ ing to kneel be _ fore my throne.*

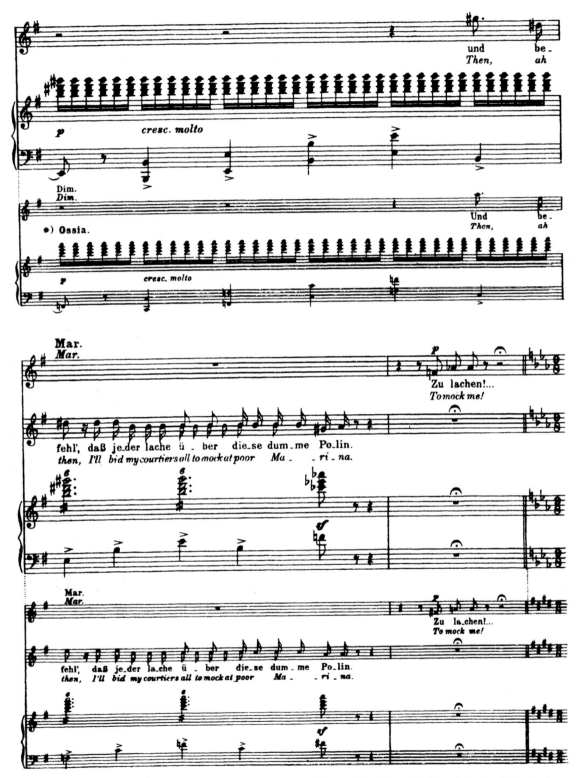

*) Variante, als Ubergang nach E-dur dienend, da von Ziffer 157 an bis zum Aktschlusse das folgende Duett auf Wunsch einen halben Ton höher (in E-dur) ausgeführt werden kann.

*Variant serving as passage to E major, because from N? 157 to the end of the act the following duet, if require, can be executed a half tone higher.*

**Duett.** | **Duet.**

**187 Larghetto amoroso.** ♩.= 50.

*dolce*

O, Za_re_witsch, ich_ be_schwör' dich; ver_gib_ mir gnä_dig mei_ne bö_ sen
O, Tsar_e_ vich, I__ en_treat thee; For_give_ me, friend, be_cause my cru_ el

Re_den;__ nicht als Vor_wurf soll_ten sie gel_ten, es sprach ja aus
words__ were not in_tend_ed, to be re_proa_ches! It was my great

ih_ _nen all mei_ne Lie_be,__ die Sor_ge um dei_ne__ Ruhmesgrö_ ße!
love__ that drove me to speak thus; jeal_ ous am I for thy fame and thine hon_ our!

Die_ Nacht,_____
Hear_ me,_____

**188**

Die dunk_ le Nacht, sie mö_ _ge sein mein Zeu_ _ge! O, mein Ge_
Now hear me, love, when night__ is dark and si_ lent. O, my__ be_

*poco cresc.*

**191**

du!
*King!*

(Umarmung.)
*(They embrace.)*

Herz!
*me!*

(Rangoni erscheint. Er beobachtet von weitem Dimitri und Marina.)
*(Rangoni is seen watching Dimitri and Marina from afar.)*

**191**

*f legato assai*

**Moderato maestoso.** ♩ = 100.

CORO.

Ten.

(Stimmen der zechenden Magnaten hinter der Bühne.)
*(The guests behind the scenes.)*
Bassi.

Vi.vat!
*Hurrah!*

Vi.vat!
*Hurrah!*

Vi.
*Hur*

**Moderato maestoso.** ♩ = 100.

vat!
*rah!*

Vi.vat!
*Hur rah!*

**Der Vorhang fällt.**
*Curtain.*

# Vierter Aufzug.
## Erstes Bild.

Eine Waldlichtung bei Kromy. Rechts ein Abhang und dahinter die Stadtmauer. Vom Abhang führt ein Weg quer über die Bühne Gradeaus das Walddickicht. Neben dem Abhange— ein großer Baumstumpf.

# Fourth Act.
## Scene I.

A clearing near Kromy. On the right hand rising-ground, with a path leading across the stage. In the distance the city walls. At the foot of the slope a great log.

**192**

Allegro. ♩ = 132.

(Den Abhang entlang stürmt ein Haufen Vagabunden; in ihrer Mitte der gebundene Bojar Chruschtschoff.)
*(A crowd of vagabonds rushes down the slope, in the midst of them the boyar Khroutshov in chains.)*

**193** L'istesso tempo.

( Verstopfen Chruschtschoffs Mund mit einem Lappen.)
*(Stuffing a rag into the mouth of Khroutshov.)*

(Setzen Chruschtschoff auf den Baumstumpf.)
*(They put Khroutshov on the log.)*

195

A_fim_ja! Komm', Täubchen, die Nachbarn sa_gen,
*Af_im_ya* *my darling* *the goss_ips do say*

Füll_sel: ein trok_ken Ding!
*pudding:* *on_ly dry bread.*

195

du wä_rest weit schon ü_ber hun_dert...
*You soon will reach your hundredth birth_day*

Al_so ist's nicht mehr ge_fährlich
*So, my dear, you're ve_ry safe...*

(Aus dem Haufen tritt, ächzend und hüstelnd, ein uraltes Weib hervor und humpelt zu Chruschtschoff hin.)
*(An old crone, grumbling and coughing, leaves the crowd and goes towards Khroutshkov.)*

poco acceler.

Sopr.

Hol_la! Nun hat ein Schätz_chen der Bo_jar! Man los!
*Fair maid, come sit you by this no_ble man!* *Come hith_er!*

Alti.

Man los!
*Come hith_er!*
*p cresc.*

Ten.

Ha, ha, ha,
*Ha, ha, ha,*
*p cresc.*

Bassi.

poco acceler.

poco cresc.

ha, ha, ha, ha, ha, ha, ha!
ha, ha, ha, ha, ha, ha, ha!

ha, ha, ha, ha, ha, ha, ha,   ha, ha, ha, ha, ha, ha, ha!
ha, ha, ha, ha, ha, ha, ha,   ha, ha, ha, ha, ha, ha, ha!

ha, ha, ha, ha, ha, ha, ha, ha,   ha, ha, ha, ha, ha, ha, ha!                    Nun
ha, ha, ha, ha, ha, ha, ha, ha,   ha, ha, ha, ha, ha, ha, ha!                    Now

Recht so!   Nun  laßt uns prei_sen ihn!
That's right!  Now  pay him hon_ours due

laßt uns prei_sen ihn!   He! Wei_ber, fan_get an!
pay him hon_ours due!   Hey! Let the wo_men start!

He! Ihr Wei_ber fanget  an!
Hey! let the women start!

(Der Chor stellt sich im Halbkreis vor Chruschtschoff auf.)
(The chorus forms a semi-circle around Khroutchov.)

196

'sist kein Fal_ke, der stolz schwebt am Him _ mel, 'sist kein feurig Roß, das stürmt mit dem Win _ de...
No _ fal_con is fly_ing in skies so blue, No _ swift steed rac_ing the meadows through,

(Verneigen sich.)
(*They salute him.*)

ja - ren, Heil ihm, dem Za - renknecht! Heil ihm!
*no - ble - man, Praise to our Tsar Bo - ris, Glo - ry!*

ja - ren, Heil ihm, dem Za - renknecht! Heil ihm!
*no - ble - man, Praise to our Tsar Bo - ris, Glo - ry!*

Hast in Eh - ren du stets uns ge - hal - ten ja,
*Think with what great hon - our you have treat - ed us*

Hast in Eh - ren du stets uns ge - hal - ten ja,
*Think with what great hon - our you have treat - ed us*

hast ge_pei_nigt und satt _ sam ge_quä_let uns, hast___ mit Peit _ schen
*Think, in snow and tempest, ov _ er the tractless steppe, our___ poor lads___ you*

hast ge_pei_nigt und satt _ sam ge_quä_let uns, hast mit Peit _ schen
*Think, in snow and tempest, ov _ er the tractless steppe, our poor lads___ you*

hie _ ben uns oft___ durch Hun _ ger und E _ lend ge _ trie _ ben.___
*drove___ like beasts of___ bur _ den; the whip was ne _ ver spared.___*

hie _ ben uns oft durch Hun _ ger und E _ lend ge _ trie _ ben.___
*drove___ like beasts of bur _ den; the whip was ne _ ver spared.___*

seht auf dem Kopf den ei _ ser _ nen Topf!
old sauce_pan cap, Ha! old sauce_pan cap!

U _ lu _ lu _ lu _ lu _ lu
Ou _ lyou _ lyou _ lyou _ lyou _ lyou.

lu _ lu _ lu _ lu _ lu _ lu,
lyou _ lyou _ lyou _ lyou _ lyou _ lyou

Trrr!
Trr!

**Andante.** ♩ = 66.

**202** **Der Blödsinnige** (setzt sich auf einen Stein und singt, hin und her schwankend).
**The Simpleton.** (The simpleton, seated on a stone, sings and rocks himself to and fro.)

Blei _ cher Mond _ schein, ein
In the moon _ light the

Kätz_chen wim_mert. Du blö_der Narr, steh auf, sprich ein frommes Sprüchlein.
cats are cry_ing, poor Sil _ ly Bil _ ly now must rise and say his prayers:

Lo _ bet Gott, den
Lord I bow in

Schöp - fer, prei - set Je - sum! Schö - nes Wet - ter wird's heut'
wor - ship, Lord I wor - ship, May it keep fine, May the

ge - ben, schö - nes Wet - ter... Mondschein....
moon shine, May the moon shine... bright - ly...

**203** Moderato. ♩ = 84.
Buben.
Sopr. *The Village boys.*

Grüß dich Gott, lie - ber, dummer Narr I - wa - nitsch! Steh auf und prei - se uns,
Good day, good day, Old Sil - ly Bil - ly, good day! Rise, pay us hon - our due,

Alti.

**203** Moderato. ♩ = 84.

tief vor uns ver - nei - ge dich! Nimm dein Mützchen ab, Mützchen ist so schwer.
Come, get up and make your bow, and doff your i - ron cap, doff your i - ron cap!

**Der Blödsinnige.**
*The Simpleton.*

Vaterland, es stöh_net un_term Druck des Gottes_leugners, un_ter der ver_fluchten Hand des Za_ren_
Rus_sia, yea groan be_neath the heel of this a_postate, weep beneath the rule of this ac_cursèd

Vaterland, es stöh_net un_term Druck des Gottes_leugners, un_ter der ver_fluchten Hand des Za_ren_
Rus_sia, yea groan be_neath the heel of this a_postate, weep beneath the rule of this ac_cursèd

mör_ders als_ Süh_ne der un_tilg_ba_ren Mis_se_tat.
reg_i_cide, to the fame of his crime still un_par_don_èd.

mör_ders als_ Süh_ne der un_tilg_ba_ren Mis_se_tat.
reg_i_cide, to the fame of his crime still un_par_don_èd.

CORO.

Sopr.

Hai_
Haï

Alti.

Ten.

Hai_
Haï

Bassi.

cresc.

mör _ _ _ der, dem Za _ ren _ mör _ der Tod!
reg _ _ i _ cide! A _ rise and slay Bo _ ris!_

mör _ _ _ der, dem Za _ ren _ mör _ der Tod!
reg _ _ i _ cide! A _ rise and slay Bo _ ris!_

mör _ _ _ der, dem Za _ ren _ mör _ der Tod!
reg _ _ i _ cide! A _ rise and slay Bo _ ris!_

mör _ _ _ der, dem Za _ ren _ mör _ der Tod!
reg _ _ i _ cide! A _ rise and slay Bo _ ris!_

**Lowitzky und Tschernjakowsky.** (hinter der Bühne).
*Lovitski and Tcherniakovsi (off the stage).*

**213** **Allegro moderato.** ♩=92.

Do _ mi _ ne, Do _ mi _ ne, sal _ vum fac Re _ _ gem, Re _ _ gem,

Re _ gem Demetrium Mos _ co _ vi _ ae, sal _ vum fac, sal _ vum fac Regem De _ metri _ um

om - nis Rus - si - ae, sal - vum fac, sal - vum fac Re - gem De - me - tri - um...

**214 CORO.**
Bassi.

Zum Teu - fel noch! Wer kommt denn da noch her?
*What men are these? What the dev - il do they here?*

Low. und Tschernj.
*Lov. and Tcher.*

Sopr.

Do - mi - ne, Do - mi - ne, sal - vum fac

Heu - len wie die Wöl - fe!
*Howl - ing worse than wolves!*

Alti.

(Laufen nach links, den Jesuiten entgegen.)
*(They run to the left, chasing the Jesuits.)*

Ten.

Was für'n Teu - felspack!
*Now! Black dev - ils?*

Warl.
*Varl.*

**215**

Low. und Tschernj. (näher kommend).
*Lov. and Tcker.*

O, die ek - le Rabenbrut! erfrecht sich
*Black crows and scavengers! They, like*

sal - vum fac, sal - vum fac, sal - vum fac.

**215**

(Die auf der Bühne nachgebliebenen Vagabunden lauschen gespannt. Krieger treten auf. Die Vagabunden kehren wieder auf die Bühne zurück.)
(A crowd of vagabonds appear upon the scene to listen. A procession of the troops of the False Demetrius passes by, after which the vagabonds occupy the scene again.)

Preis dir und Ruhm,_____ Dmi _ tri I _ wa _ nowitsch!
*Glo _ ry to thee!* *Whom God has saved to us!*

Preis dir und Ruhm,_____ Dmi _ tri I _ wa _ nowitsch!
*Glo _ ry to thee!* *Whom God has saved to us!*

I.

*cresc. sempre*

**222** (Hoch zu Roß erscheint der falsche Demetrius.)
*(The False Dimitri appears on horseback.)*

Heil dir und Se _ gen, Di _ mi _ tri I _ wa _ nowitsch! Heil_____ dir,
*Long life and glo _ ry,* *Di _ mi _ tri I _ van _ o _ vich!* *Glo _ ry.*

Heil dir und Se _ gen, Di _ mi _ tri I _ wa _ nowitsch! Heil_____ dir,
*Long life and glo _ ry,* *Di _ mi _ tri I _ van _ o _ vich!* *Glo _ ry,*

**222**

Moderato e maestoso. ♩=84.

**Der falsche Demetrius** (vom Roß herab).
**223** *The false Dimitri* (on horseback).

Wir, Di_mi_tri I_wa_nowitsch, Wir, von Got_tes Gna_den, Za_
We, Di_mi_tri I_vano_vich, By the ho_ly will of God, Tsar_

rewitsch des Reußenreiches, Fürst vom Ge_blü_te Uns_rer Ah_nen. Euch, von
e_vich of all the Russias; Prince of the blood, and law_ful ru_ler, Lo, we

Go_du_now Ver_folg_ten—— ver_kün_den Wir hiermit in Gna_den Uns_ren ho_hen
pledge our word, and promise help, and pro_tec_tion from Bo_ris, ref_uge from op_

poco rit.

(Man hört die Sturmglocke.*)
(The tocsin is heard ringing off the stage.*)

un _ ser Zar,____ Preis dir und Ruhm!____
Hail to thee,____ Tsar!____ Hail to thee!____

(Die Menge folgt dem falschen Dmitri nach.)
(The crowd follows the False Dimitri.)

un _ ser Zar, Preis dir und Ruhm!____
Hail to thee,____ Tsar!____ Hail to thee!____

Low und Tschernj. (Dem falschen Dmitri folgend.)
Lov. and Tcher. (follow Dimitri.)

De _ o____ glo _ ria,____ glo _ ria____

Wir____ fol _ gen dir,____ Di _ mi _ tri I.
Glo _ ry Hail to thee,____ Di _ mi _ tri I.

Wir____ fol _ gen dir,____ Di _ mi _ tri I.
Glo _ ry Hail to thee,____ Di _ mi _ tri I.

*) Anmerk Je zwei Schläge auf jeden Takt (bis Ziffer 226.)
*) Two beats in the bar up to 226.

**265**

(Setzt sich auf einen Stein. Von rechts her loht der Widerschein einer großen Feuersbrunst herüber.)
*seated on a stone. To the right the glow of a great fire.)*

Fließet, flie___ßet, hei___ße, bittre Tränen,
*Flow, ah!__ flow, my bit___ter__ tears,*

Wei___ne,___ recht__ gläub'ge Christenseele! Denn der Feind kommt bald und dann senkt sich
*Weep, la___ment, all ye true be.lievers! Soon the foe will come, all the world grow*

nie___der die Fin___ster___nis auf das Va___ter___land. We___he, We___he dir, du__
*dark, dark as black.est night ne'er a star shines through. Woe and sor___row al___ways! la___*

**227**

ar___mes Volk, du__ hun___gernd Volk!... Der Vorhang fällt.
*ment, Russian folk, poor hung___ry folk!__ Curtain.*

## Zweites Bild.

## Scene II.

Der große Empfangsaal im alten Zarenschlosse in Moskau. An den Seiten Bänke. Rechts der Ausgang auf die rote Freitreppe, links in die inneren Zarengemächer. Rechts, näher zur Rampe, ein Tisch mit Schreibgerät; mehr nach links der Platz für den Zaren. Außerordentliche Sitzung der Bojarenduma.

The Granovitaya Palace in the Kremlin. Benches on each side. On the right a door giving on to the Red Staircase. Also on the right, but nearer to the footlights a table with writing materials. On the left the seat of the Tsar. A special sitting of the Duma of the boyards.

Andante non troppo.

dra_len, Klöstern sei's ver_kün_det.
pub_lic place and square... by or_der.

Und knie_end soll zu Gott ge_
Com_mand the peo_ple on their

Andante non troppo.

legato assai

fle_het werden, Er mö_ge, gnädig sich er_bar_mend,
knees to sup_pli_cate and en_treat the Lord for Rus_sia,

uns Frieden schenken.
our suffring coun_try.

**234** Moderato. ♩ = 92.

(Schuiskij tritt herein.)
(Enter Shouïsky.)

Zwar ist's ein Wüh_ler, doch sei_ne
Though he's a schem_er, we can_not

Schad', Schui_skj fehlt im Ra_te.
Ill luck! Shouis_ky's not here!

**234** Moderato. ♩ = 92.

durch Zufall auf geblieben. O, was er blick't ich da, Bo ja ren!
*through a chink I spied him... O, friends I saw a fearsome sight!*

**235** Allegro moderato *(alla breve).* ♩ = 72.

Bleich, mit kal tem Schweiß be deckt und zit ternd am gan zen
*Pal lid, an ic y sweat up on this brow, his whole frame*

Lei be, und murmelnd dumpf und wirr gar seltsam ab ge riss' ne Wor te,
*shak ing, the Tsar was babbling low, such strange unmeaning words and phra ses,*

flam men de Wut in den Blik ken... saß da der Zar, in
*While his eyes were flash ing with frenz y! Some dark and dead ly*

gräß li chen Qua len, in fürch ter li cher Angst sich win dend.
*se cret de vours him; Bo ris by con stant an guish is bro ken.*

**236**

Bleich, wie der Tod, wild starrend in die Ek_ke, und stöh_nend vor töd_lichem Ent_
*Then, turn_ing pale, as though he saw some spectre, he cried a_loud and bade the thing de-*

set_zen... Laut fle_hend zum er_mor_de_ten Za_re_witsch,
*part! T'was the Tsar_e_vich who ap_pear'd, as though to haunt_ him.*

Ha! das lügst du!
*No! not so, Prince!*

**237** (Zar Boris tritt herein.)
*(Enter Boris.)*

sein bleich Ge_spenst voll grausger Angst ab_weh_rend... „Fort!"
*Vain_ly, then, Bo_ris im_plored for mer_cy, cry_ing "a_vaunt!" "a*

Was?
*What?*

Sieh er - bar - mend her - nie - der!
*May the Saints pro - tect us!*

A.

**Boris.** (Sich der Rampe nähernd.)
*Boris.* (*Approaching the footlights.*)

**238** Andante. ♩=♩

Fort, fort...
*vaunt! A - vaunt!*

Wer sagt, ich sei der Mörder?... Es ist nicht wahr! Es lebt, das Kind!
*What voice said "Thou murd'rer? No murd'rer I! Boy, thou still liovest!*

Und Schuiskij soll für sei - ne Lü - gen - re - den gevierteilt
*And Shouïs - ky de - serves for his false oath some awful*

Wer weiß, viel _ leicht wird des Grei _ sen fromm Ge _ spräch heil _ sam
Per _ chance to talk with this an _ cient man of God may re _

lin _ dern mei _ ner See _ le Trau _ rigkeit und Angst!...
store my peace of mind and bring my soul re _ pose!...

### Pimens Erzählung. | Pimen's Tale.

Andante. ♩ = 72.

**241**

Pimen. (Pimen tritt herein und bleibt, Boris scharf anblickend, stehen.)
Pimen. (Enter Pimen, who stands before Boris and looks fixedly at him.)

Ein
A

from _ mer Die _ ner des Herrn bin ich, der längst ent _ sagt der Welt. Ich
peace _ ful monk, who know _ eth nought of world _ ly lore and wisdom, now

**248** Andante. ♩=72.

Leb wohl, mein Sohn, o, ich ster_be... und bald wirst
*Farewell, my son, I am dy_ing. 'Tis thou wilt*

du der Zar nun sein. O fra_ge nicht, auf wel_che Weis' ich
*reign when I am gone. Enquire thou not how to thy fa_ther*

Zar gewor_den bin; nicht sollst es wis_sen du. Du wirst als rech_ter
*came the Russian throne, for it concerns thee not. Thou art a true and*

Zar re_gie_ren, als mein Za_rewitsch, als erst_ge_bor_ner Sohn.
*law_ful Tsar, Thou art my heir, thou art my el_dest son.*

Hör' mich, mein Kind, mein heiß_ge_lieb_tes!
*Dear son, thy fa_ther's well be_lov_ed!*

249 **Allegro moderato.** ♩ = 112.

Trau – e nicht den Bo – ja – ren, mein Sohn, den fal – schen;
*Be thou cau – tious and trust not too much the no – bles;*

scharf späh' nach ih – rem Ein – ver – ständ – nis, dem heim – li – chen mit Lit – tau'n;
*Watch all their plot – tings, their se – cret in – trigues with Lith – u – an – ia;*

den Lan – des – ver – rat mußt du stra – fen er – barmungs – los und streng;
*Chas – tize all the trai – tors with ri – gour, and show not an – y mer – cy;*

hal – te auf stren – ges Ge – richt, doch stets gerecht und wei – se. Ste – he stets auf der Wacht des
*prove thy – self just to the peo – ple, firm and im – par – tial. Be the champion and guardian of*

*mf sempre*

rech – ten, heil' – gen Glaubens, fromm ver – eh – re stets die Hei – li – gen Got – tes. Be –
*Rus – sia's Ho – ly Church; hon – our all the bles – sèd Saints of God.____ My*

250 Meno mosso. ♩ = 84.

hü - te treu, mein Sohn, dein lie - bes Schwester - lein; du blei - best nun der ein - zi - ge Be -
son, protect thy sis - ter, our Tsa - rev - na, She has but thee to care for her on

schüt - zer uns - rer Xe - nia, uns - rer rei - nen Tau - be.
earth; — Cher - ish her, my pure and spot - less dove. —

(beinah sprechend)
(almost parlando)

O, mein Gott! o, mein Gott! ich fleh' dich an, o sei ein
God in Heav'n! O my God! Thou see - st me, how I, a

gnäd'ger Rich - ter mir... o, sieh er - barmungsvoll auf mei - ne Va - ter - trä - nen!...
sin - ful fa - ther pray with tears for this my son! Not for my - self, o God!

(Kirchensänger hinter der Bühne.)
(Behind the scenes.)

die To _ ten _
The mourner's

CORO.

**Sopr.**
pp — unis. —
Wei _ net, all ihr Sterb _ li _ chen,      denn das Le _ ben
All ye peo _ ple, weep, la _ ment!      For he breathes no

**Alti.**
pp

**Ten.**
pp
Wei _ net, all ihr Sterb _ li _ chen,      denn das Le _ ben
All ye peo _ ple, weep, la _ ment!      For he breathes no

**Bassi.**
pp

morendo          p

Klag !      Gebt mir    das heil'ge Mönchskleid. . . .   in's Klo _ ster geht der Zar.
cry:      "Wrap him  in monks at _ tire      and bear  the Tsar  a _ way"

flieht    und bald    kommt die  Gra _ bes _ nacht  und das ew' _ ge Schwei _
more;    His lips    are for    ev _ er seal'd,  And no  an _ swer may  he

flieht    und bald    kommt die  Gra _ bes _ nacht  und das ew' _ ge Schwei _
more;    His lips    are for    ev _ er seal'd,  And no  an _ swer may  he

(Kirchensänger hinter der Bühne.)
(Behind the scenes.)

CORO.

Sopr.

Weinet, all ihr Sterb.li.chen, denn das Le_ben
All ye peo_ple, weep, la_ment! For he breathes no

Alti.

Ten.

Weinet, all ihr Sterb.li.chen, denn das Le_ben
All ye peo_ple, weep, la_ment! For he breathes no

Bassi.

die To_ten_
The mourner's

morendo

Klag! Gebt mir das heil'geMönchskleid.... in's Klo_ster geht der Zar.
cry: "Wrap him in monks at_tire and bear the Tsar a_way"

flieht und bald kommt die Gra_bes_nacht und das ew'ge Schwei_
more; His lips are for ev_er seal'd, And no an_swer may he

flieht und bald kommt die Gra_bes_nacht und das ew'ge Schwei_
more; His lips are for ev_er seal'd, And no an_swer may he